A HISTORY OF U.S. FEMINISMS

A HISTORY OF U.S. FEMINISMS

RORY DICKER

SEAL PRESS

A History of U.S. Feminisms
© 2016, 2008 Rory Dicker

Published by Seal Press
a member of the Perseus Books Group
1700 Fourth Street
Berkeley, CA 94710

Library of Congress Cataloging-in-Publication Data

Dicker, Rory Cooke, 1969-
A history of U.S. feminisms / by Rory Dicker.
    p. cm.
ISBN-13: 978-1-58005-588-8
1. Feminism—United States—History. 2. Women's rights—United States—History. 3. Women—United States—History. I. Title.
HQ1420.D55 2008
305.420973—dc22

                    2008005241

Cover design by Tim Green, Faceout Studio
Cover photos (top left) © Hulton Archive / Staff/Getty Images; (top right and lower left) Wikimedia Commons; (bottom right) © Liora K Photography, http://www.liorak photography.com/

Book design by Mike Walters
Printed in the United States of America
Distributed by Publishers Group West

10 9 8 7 6 5 4 3 2 1

For Saul Dicker
(1940–2007)

CONTENTS

PREFACE

A LOT HAS CHANGED IN THE FEMINIST LANDSCAPE since the first edition of *A History of U.S. Feminisms* appeared in 2008. To state the most obvious, Hillary Clinton campaigned for the Democratic nomination for president in 2008; she is seeking the nomination in the 2016 election as I write this. Barack Obama, the man who received the Democratic nomination and became president for two terms, has shown his support of feminism in various ways. The Lilly Ledbetter Fair Pay Act of 2009, the first significant legislation signed by President Obama, helps protect individuals against pay discrimination; in addition, the president has made policies such as affordable childcare and mandatory paid family leave a part of his State of the Union addresses. President Obama's commitment to ending sexual assault on college campuses has led to a stricter enforcement of Title IX, the law that protects people from sex discrimination at educational institutions receiving federal funding. The Obama administration created the White House Task Force to Protect Students from Sexual Assault and launched the "It's On Us" public awareness and education campaign, which asks people to prevent sexual assault by developing new social norms about masculinity and bystander intervention.

Perhaps because I have two young daughters, I notice the ways society has started to show more concern about the experience of girls, not just in terms of sexual assault, but in terms of girls' intellectual development and their growth in confidence. Although this may be a trivial example, the popularity of the Disney film *Frozen* indicates that young girls, tweens, and their parents crave movies that feature relationships between female characters. Even though it is marketed as just another Disney princess movie, the film is different: in this movie, Prince Charming turns out to be a schemer, romantic love is not the focus, and sisterhood is powerful. Indeed, the love story of the two sisters is what is most central to the narrative. Like *Frozen*, other recent cultural creations show a desire to take girls—both young and adolescent—seriously. Not long before I saw *Frozen* in early 2014, I heard about GoldieBlox, a toy company that, by encouraging girls' interest in building and designing structures, hopes to address the underrepresentation of females in STEM (science, technology, engineering, and mathematics) fields. An ad for GoldieBlox and the Spinning Machine depicts three girls delighting in the construction of a Rube Goldberg machine in their house, garage, driveway, and yard. The ad's soundtrack, an unauthorized remake of the Beastie Boys' "Girls," asserts that girls are tired of "pink and pretty" playthings and instead "deserve to see a range" of toys, particularly those that allow them "to use [their] brains." Although GoldieBlox is packaged in pink, its goal is to value girls for their intellect and their potential as problem-solvers. Another product for girls, this one aimed at teenagers, is *Rookie*, an online magazine launched in September 2011; through its features that focus on everything from astronomy and camping to manicures and flower arranging, the magazine illustrates that it is okay for girls to be interested in both femininity and feminism. *Rookie* affirms girls' wide-ranging interests as part of a process of self-discovery.

Just as some parts of the culture are focusing on girls, commitments to difference and equality feel more central to daily life than ever before. For instance, public opinion of same-sex marriage has shifted in the last ten years, from 36 percent in favor in 2005 to around 60 percent in favor in 2015. President Obama's endorsement of marriage equality in 2012 may have helped change some people's perceptions on the issue, but the Supreme Court's ruling in 2013 against a key part of the Defense of Marriage Act has led to real changes for gay couples, who are now able to access the same federal benefits received by straight couples. Furthermore, the Supreme Court's ruling in *Obergefell v. Hodges* in 2015 legalized same-sex marriages in all fifty states. Gay and lesbian members of the armed services felt real effects, too, when the Don't Ask, Don't Tell policy mandating the hiding of sexual orientation at the risk of being discharged was repealed in 2010. The presence of transgendered individuals in the news media and popular culture—Laverne Cox, Janet Mock, Chelsea Manning, and, most recently, Caitlyn Jenner—has led to a greater awareness among the general public of the inequality experienced by people whose bodies do not match their internal sense of their gender. The term "cisgender," which refers to a person whose understanding of their gender aligns with the sex they were assigned at birth, is used with more frequency now than it was in 2008, when this book was first published.

Although there has seemed to be a groundswell of support for trans and gay rights, in other ways, American society seems to be moving backward. The repeated killings of unarmed black men—Trayvon Martin, Eric Garner, Michael Brown, Freddie Gray, to name only the most prominent ones—by neighborhood vigilantes or police officers smacks of Jim Crow-era injustice at a time when the United States has its first black president. Even though he was not shot or killed by the authorities, the case of Kalief Browder, a black teenager arrested for stealing a backpack and held at Rikers Island jail without trial for three years, almost two of which were spent in solitary confinement, received attention when it was the subject of a profile in *The New Yorker*. Although Browder was released in 2013, despair from his treatment and all he had lost during his three years of captivity led him to take his own life in 2015. In response to the way mainstream society seems to consider black people unimportant and meaningless, the #BlackLivesMatter movement, begun in 2013, protests the structural racism that leads to police brutality, the mass incarceration of black men, and the belief that black people are disposable.

A different example of society seeming to regress has to do with reproductive rights. When Sandra Fluke, then a student at Georgetown

Law School, testified in 2012 before the House Democratic Steering and Policy Committee about why Georgetown—a Catholic institution—should provide health care coverage for contraceptive drugs, the conservative radio host Rush Limbaugh called her a "slut" and a "prostitute." Limbaugh's comment was hardly an isolated one; a couple of months earlier, Foster Friess, a donor supporting Rick Santorum's bid for the presidency, stated that, when he was young, women "used Bayer aspirin for contraception. The gals put it between their knees, and it wasn't that costly." Because of remarks such as these, some referred to a Republican "War on Women" in 2012, a war that moved beyond vitriol and included the discussion or passage in state legislatures of bills that would restrict access to abortion, including those that would force women to undergo an invasive transvaginal ultrasound before they could have an abortion. Another state legislator, Joe Walsh, a Republican congressman from Illinois, added to this "war" by declaring that abortions are "absolutely" never medically necessary to save the life of a woman: "With modern technology and science," he averred, "you can't find one instance. There is no such exception as life of the mother, and as far as health of the mother, same thing." Although comments such as these were criticized immediately and even had political repercussions for those who made them, the clear antifeminist subtext of these statements was hard to miss. For example, when Todd Akin, a Republican candidate for the U.S. Senate from Missouri, shared his views on abortion and stated that "legitimate rape rarely leads to pregnancy," he quickly lost support for his Senate campaign; his statement revealed a kind of ranking of sexual assault which did not sit well with victims, advocates, or feminists.

The publicity surrounding several cases of sexual assault offered another example of a kind of "war" on women and girls. The documentary *The Invisible War* (2012) describes the prevalence of rape in the U.S. military, and discusses how few rapes are reported and even fewer are prosecuted or punished. The film's narration of the stories of individual women—and men—reveals the harm done to subordinates by a system that values hierarchy, authority, and obedience. The rape of a teenage girl in Steubenville, Ohio, in the summer of 2012 brought attention to a high school sports culture that, like the military, seemed to accept not just the sexual violation of a drunk teenage girl but the filming and photographing of this violation and the subsequent sharing of photos of the act with friends through social media. The trial of the two football players accused and convicted of the crime revealed text messages and pictures posted to sites such as Twitter, Facebook, and YouTube. As disturbing as these texts and images were, equally disheartening was the trial's media coverage, which tended to downplay any feelings for the victim and instead offered sympathy to the rapists, who lost "promising futures" because of the trial. The rape that occurred at my own institution, Vanderbilt University, the summer after the Steubenville verdict, seemed eerily reminiscent of the Ohio crime. In June 2013, four members of the football team sexually assaulted an unconscious Vanderbilt student they carried into a dorm room after returning to campus from a downtown bar, where all had been partying. As in the Steubenville cases, the rapists shared their actions with friends by taking pictures and sending text messages. The dehumanization of the victim shocked the campus community, and the rape case and ensuing trial received a great deal of local and national media attention.

Taken together, these developments make it feel as if American society is less enlightened, more hostile to equality than ever. I would be utterly despondent if I didn't also teach young people who are passionately engaged about a range of feminist issues. Through them, I realize that today's college students care deeply about feminism and want to work to make American society more equitable for everyone. I have noticed a kind of excitement among certain students, as if they are just learning about the power and possibilities of feminism as a set of beliefs and social commitments. These students reject the idea that society is regressing beyond repair. For these students, there is a feeling of intense activist energy, a desire to see where feminist social engagement will take them. The activist Shelby Knox explains that the millennial generation has a relationship to feminism that is different from the relationship of those in Generation X. Knox states that, because of "the regression of gender roles after 9/11..., it's more of a *discovery* of feminism . . . than an *inheritance*" of it. This distinction is important because it suggests that, just as younger people aren't weighed down by a feminist ideal they have to live up to or imitate, they are equally ready to learn about feminism and to reinvent it for themselves. This sense of discovery dovetails with my own desire to teach the history of feminism, to ensure that younger people understand what came before them and how their present experiences of equality—and inequality— are shaped by earlier feminist successes and failures.

For this reason, I was excited to see *Makers*, a documentary about the women's movement in the United States that premiered on PBS in 2013. The three-part series first shows the experiences of women in the 1950s and early 1960s, before second wave feminism began, and then examines the women's movement of the 1960s and 1970s and its aftermath in the 1980s and 1990s. Although the documentary doesn't represent contemporary feminism fully or even accurately, its portrayal of second wave feminism includes much detail, such as footage from the Miss America Protest and the sit-in at the *Ladies' Home Journal*. Because of this detail and an excellent website full of supplementary interviews, I use *Makers* in my teaching; in fact, the first semester after the film appeared I felt practically giddy when I was able to share segments from the film with students in my class on contemporary women's movements.

As much as I admire and appreciate *Makers*, I wonder about its title, which seems safe and almost euphemistic. The title *Makers: Women Who Make America* seems to mask the fact that this is a film about contemporary feminist history. Why does this information need to be veiled? Shouldn't it be stated more overtly? Why isn't the film's real subject—the history of the women's movement—announced more explicitly and proudly? I understand, of course, that the creators of the film probably avoided the word "feminism" because of the word's negative connotations. They may have worried that a title that included the word "feminist" would alienate potential viewers. After all, in her interview on *Makers*, Marissa Mayer, the president and Chief Executive Officer of Yahoo, stated: "I don't think that I would consider myself a feminist. I think that I certainly believe in equal rights. I believe that women are just as capable, if not more so, in a lot of different dimensions. But I don't, I think, have sort of the militant drive and sort of the chip on the shoulder that sometimes comes with that." Mayer's rejection of the label "feminist" prompted the writer Hannah Rosin to rethink her allegiance to the term; in an article in *Slate*, Rosin writes that "insisting on the term 'feminism' may be getting in the way of fighting" the battles that women need to fight today.

I am not ready to give up on the term "feminism," however. I understand, of course, that there is an undeniable reluctance on the part of Americans to claim the term, to own it. A recent HuffPost/YouGov poll found that only 20 percent of Americans would call themselves a feminist, though 82 percent agreed that "men and women should be social, political, and economic equals." Given American society's skittishness about the term "feminism," it is hardly surprising that *Makers* did not label itself a film about feminist history.

What is surprising, though, and refreshing and wonderful, is to see prominent people who are unafraid to claim the term for themselves, and to start explaining its meaning to others. Sheryl Sandberg does so in her bestselling book *Lean In*; the actress Emma Watson declared her feminism as she launched the "HeForShe" campaign at the United Nations in 2014. Also in 2014, the actor Joseph Gordon-Levitt made "Re: Feminism," a short, accessible, and engaging video explaining his belief in feminism, and posted it on hitRECord, his online collaborative production company. Beyoncé's song "Flawless" (2013) samples sections from Chimamanda Ngozi Adichie's TED talk "We Should All Be Feminists," and when Beyoncé performed at the MTV Video Music Awards in 2014, she stood in front of a screen with the word "feminist" printed in enormous capital letters while parts of Adichie's talk played. Although she is less well known than Beyoncé, Adichie, a Nigerian writer, offers a compelling definition of a feminist in her talk. She states that, to her, a feminist is "a man or a woman who says, 'yes, there's a problem with gender as it is today, and we must fix it, we must do better.'" In Adichie's other, equally famous, TED talk, "The Danger of a Single Story," she argues that we need to be wary of "single stories"; having only one story about a group of people, of an ethnic group, of a country, or of a continent—to use Adichie's example of Africa—means that people don't learn the particular details that make individuals, groups, and places distinctive. According to Adichie, "The single story creates stereotypes, and the problem with stereotypes is not that they are untrue, but that they are incomplete."

Single stories about feminism are incomplete and, even, dangerous. By talking about feminism, learning about its history, explaining what it means and what it can help us do, we can uncover the real meaning of the term and ask new questions of feminist movement. We don't have to fear those with a "militant drive" or a "chip on their shoulder." Instead, we can try to understand feminism's abilities to dismantle systems of privilege, domination, and oppression. We can embrace the energy and anger Adichie discusses in her TED talk about feminism while also remaining hopeful about people's abilities—using the tools of dialogue and story sharing—to change society.

PROLOGUE

I AM A RELATIVE LATECOMER TO FEMINISM. I did not embrace feminism or call myself a feminist until I was in my midtwenties. As strange as this reality seems to me now, it makes some sense: I am a product of both the feminist successes of the 1960s and '70s and the backlash rhetoric of the 1980s. This meant a couple of things: First, I grew up hearing little about traditional gender role expectations for me as a girl and much about my abilities to accomplish whatever I set my mind to. Second, I imbibed the culture's hostility to feminism; even though I didn't really know what the "f-word" was, I recognized it as something dangerous. Because I was a studious, "good" girl intent on following the rules, I didn't try to find out the word's meaning for myself.

Thanks to my parents and to a culture influenced by feminism, I grew up believing that I could be and do anything. Although I come from a traditional middle-class family—my father was, until he retired, a high school English teacher and my mother, though trained as an elementary school teacher, has not worked outside the home since I was born—my parents never seemed concerned that their children replicate the roles they assumed in their marriage and their lives. Indeed, when I was growing up, my parents never indicated their wish for me to "settle down"; they expressed these hopes only when I was in my late twenties and still single. Mainly, I recall my parents treating me as someone whose goals and aspirations should be serious and taken seriously. They wanted me to study what I enjoyed and what I was good at; they didn't expect a lucrative career for me in return, but they didn't expect I would be taken care of by a husband, either. This approach to parenting seems pretty feminist to me.

My college education gave me a solid grounding in the liberal arts, but it didn't "radicalize" me in any real sense. A serious student, I took hardcore literature courses, in both English and French. During my sophomore year, I read *The Mill on the Floss, Anna Karenina,* and *Madame Bovary* in one of my classes; the lives of these novels' heroines fascinated me, but I did not think of gender as the link among these characters. As I read in college—and later graduate school—female protagonists were most compelling to me; yet, until I got to grad school, I did not seek out female writers to study. I didn't take any women's studies courses as an undergraduate, either; I'm not even sure whether my university had such a program or department.

Part of my distance from feminism sprang from an ignorance certainly shaped in some inchoate way by cultural attitudes toward feminism. When my older sister, then in college, went through a brief radical feminist "phase"—not shaving her legs or armpits, questioning the Catholic Church's exclusion of women, agitating against the antiabortion group Operation Rescue, whose founder lived in her college town—I didn't know how to interpret her behavior. Instead of wondering why she was rebelling, I categorized her as odd, a fringe-dweller. I was content to keep my head safely inside books; I rarely engaged with current events, though I am happy to say that I voted for the first time in the 1988 presidential election, for Dukakis, no less.

Even after my college graduation, it took a while for me to call myself a feminist. At my first full-time job, at a publishing company, I admired the steady work ethic of my bosses, one a single, childless woman, the other a married woman with teenage children. Unlike these women, the company's managing editor—and my bosses' boss—was a disorganized, frazzled woman, the stereotypical "Superwoman" who tries to do everything. In her case, she often failed, missing meetings and deadlines and speaking abruptly and even cruelly to her underlings. Because I was so young, I never thought about the realities of her life: The mother of a toddler, she faced many demands as she juggled her family and career, and she had no one to model herself on; as one of the highest-ranking women in the company, she was a trailblazer. Yet, I didn't see any of this; instead, I blamed her for the chaos and disorder that surrounded her, unable to understand that any social or institutional forces could be at work in making her life as hard as it was.

It was only when I got to graduate school that I started to come closer to feminism, mainly through my study of nineteenth-century American women writers. As I read long-forgotten female authors and learned about their lives, I realized that these women faced obstacles I could only imagine: They didn't have the advantages of the education I took for granted, and they were expected to marry, live quietly, and have many, many children. In a number of classes and independent studies, I pieced together some crucial details of American women's history. Sad as it may be, my appreciation of these women's lives pushed me toward feminism more directly than did any engagement with current events or "real life."

As I started to self-identify as a feminist, I grew more involved in the teaching of women's and gender studies classes. In my first job out of graduate school I helped to set up a women's and gender studies minor at a small liberal arts college; the strategic work of planning the minor and figuring out a way of explaining it to the committee that would grant its approval gave me an appreciation for the delicate and challenging work performed by the people who set up pioneering women's studies programs thirty years before.

In the past few years, in my introductory women's and gender studies classes, I have taught Katja von Garnier's film *Iron Jawed Angels,* which chronicles the last decade of the American campaign for women's suffrage. For many students, viewing this film replicates the experience I had learning about American women's history: When they discover the inequalities women faced in the past, students can't help calling themselves feminists. I hope reading this brief history of feminism in the United States has a similar effect on you.

CHAPTER 1

FEMINISM'S LEGACY

LAST WEEK, THREE SEPARATE INCIDENTS OCCURRING within the space of about two hours reminded me in powerful ways what feminism has accomplished in American culture and why it is as urgently needed now as it ever was.

As I stood in line at a deli waiting to place a to-go order, I overheard snippets of a conversation between two people I assumed were mother and daughter. The mother made repeated suggestions of what the daughter might have for lunch, but the daughter rejected each idea, insisting that she did not like the place's food. My interest piqued by such a blanket claim about a deli whose food is quite good, I turned and in one glance understood all: Toothpick arms were folded protectively across a gaunt body dressed in a short skirt and T-shirt. Even the horizontal stripes of her shirt did not give the teenager's emaciated body any heft; smiling quietly, the mother endured her daughter's complaints as if used to them. I turned away. Although I routinely discuss eating disorders in the classes I teach, witnessing such a body filled me with both sadness and rage.

After lunch, which I ate hungrily, a coworker told me about a mutual acquaintance whose boss had abruptly dropped on her desk a letter in which he asked her when she planned to stop breastfeeding her infant daughter. Although her child is in daycare, this woman uses a breast pump at work to maintain her milk supply. And even though the woman is able to continue working while she pumps—indeed, her productivity has not declined while she has been nursing her child—her male boss, perhaps because he felt uncomfortable about her pumping behind the closed doors of her office or because he wanted to exert some kind of control over her, made remarks that caused this woman stress and unhappiness, not to mention concern about the security of her job.

Later, as I walked down the street to pick up my daughter from childcare, I ran into a friend who asked if I'd seen the newspaper story about a grad student we both knew. I hadn't, so my friend explained that this woman had just filed a sexual harassment lawsuit against her dissertation director. According to the woman's allegations, the professor manifested his misogyny by saying that women are good only for sex; he expected his student to find female sexual partners for him, and if she didn't, he would not continue to support her research. Stating that this professor had hindered her career, this woman first filed a claim with the Equal Employment Opportunity Commission (EEOC) and then launched a suit against the faculty member and the university.

These incidents jolted me awake—it's not every day that I am barraged with so many examples of our patriarchal culture's hatred of women. As I reflected on what I saw and heard, I realized one thing all of these women had in common: All were quite young, ranging in age from about sixteen to thirty. These women had so much to look forward to in life, and here they were, stymied by entrenched norms about what women should or shouldn't be, do, or look like. Part of me grew despondent as I considered the costs—emotional, physical, psychological, economic—of being female in American society.

Yet, as I thought about these examples of patriarchy's reign, I recognized my indebtedness to feminism, which has given me not just the language to talk about the sexism I witness but the tools to analyze and understand it. Feminists of the second wave—the women's movement occurring in the 1960s and '70s—invented words such as "sexism" and "sexual harassment," and it was during the heyday of the second wave that behavior such as that of the antibreastfeeding boss was labeled "sex discrimination" and deemed illegal. Because of the work of feminists, the graduate student could file a complaint with the EEOC and the young mother could submit a grievance at her workplace. In addition, the clinical and written work of feminist psychologists, psychiatrists, and social workers has saved the lives of countless young women plagued by eating disorders and educated their families and the general public about these devastating illnesses. These examples remind me that feminism has made valuable, concrete changes to the lives of women and men in this country. In spite of these changes, feminism is still needed, among other reasons, to ensure that women are treated fairly in school and on the job and to critique and correct a culture that mandates a homogeneous beauty ideal for all women. It is also needed—and these are no mean feats—to protect women's reproductive rights and to eradicate sexism.

What, then, is feminism, and why don't more people understand it for what it is? In the last fifteen years, I have taught countless introductory women's and gender studies classes, and I

Classic feminist cartoon. Artist and date unknown.

am constantly disabusing students of their caricatured impressions of feminism and feminists. When I ask students to describe what they imagine when they hear the word "feminist," in short order they are able to rattle off all of the often-invoked stereotypes. They tell me that a feminist is ugly, hairy, and wears no makeup. She is a man-hating, butch lesbian. She is violent, angry, and humorless, rushing from one protest to the next. Constantly policing her own behavior along with that of her family, friends, and colleagues, she is, to use Rush Limbaugh's famous neologism, a "feminazi."

After hearing this litany, I do two things. First, I tell my students that I am a feminist. Startled that a feminist could be packaged as I am—a petite white heterosexual woman who smiles and has been known to wear lipstick—students then listen as I read a standard definition of "feminism," such as this one from *The American Heritage Dictionary:* Feminism is the "belief in the social, political, and economic equality of the sexes" as well as the "movement organized around this belief." We talk about this definition, and many students begin to realize that, even if they had never thought so before, they are feminists. How could they not support a principle as American as "equality"? Our discussion then moves on to why, even though they know so little about what feminism actually is, they have such distorted images of what a feminist looks like. We talk about the media's perpetuation of the feminist stereotype, referring to various filmic incarnations, such as Enid, the serious-looking law student in *Legally Blonde,* who holds a PhD in women's studies with an "emphasis in the History of Combat." I have students read the chapter from Susan Douglas's *Where the Girls Are* about the media's coverage of the women's movement in the late 1960s and early '70s so they can understand how current stereotypical images of feminists were deliberately constructed by a media culture antagonistic to many of feminism's demands.

Like Douglas's chapter, much of the material students read at the start of my introductory course emphasizes the importance of history. Women did not always have the rights they enjoy today, and it is crucial to learn about how women—and men—fought to change a society that, in spite of its talk about equality, disenfranchised the female sex until the ratification of the Nineteenth Amendment in 1920. Unless we read and study the history of women's rights, we run the risk of forgetting what actually happened to women in the past, how they were treated, and how they were taught to think about themselves. My belief that people need to understand the history of feminism in the United States prompted me to write this book; in no way an exhaustive history, it sketches out the parameters of American feminist history so that readers can understand what feminism really is, what feminists believe, and what feminists have accomplished.

So much of what we take for granted in our everyday lives we owe to people who believed that women deserved to be treated equally in

Riding Feminism's Waves

Although second wavers started to call themselves feminists in the late 1960s, they did not initially think of their work as another "wave" of the women's movement. At least initially, the language of "waves" served the purposes of the historian rather than of the participants in the women's movement. Women's rights activists in the nineteenth and early twentieth centuries certainly did not recognize the need for such terminology; they were trailblazers of the movement and thus did not know where it would go or how it would progress.

The conceptualization of feminism in terms of waves seems to have first appeared in March 1968, when Martha Lear wrote an article for the *New York Times Magazine* in which she referred to a "second feminist wave." As the second wave progressed and women's history developed as an academic specialty in the 1970s, feminists began to trace their connections to the activists who preceded them, referring to their precursors as the first wave and themselves as the second. These days, the terminology is commonplace.

In *Moving the Mountain: The Women's Movement in America Since 1960,* Flora Davis explains the usefulness of the wave metaphor for describing how social change occurs: "First, there's a lot of intense activity and some aspects of life are transformed; then . . . reaction sets in. Stability reigns for a while, and if there's a strong backlash, some of the changes may be undone. Eventually, if vital issues remain unresolved, another wave of activism arises."

The wave metaphor has been meaningful because it captures the forward and backward movement, the ebb and flow, of feminism. As feminist agitation has yielded some social changes, some segments of society have reacted against the changes, stalling forward momentum. The idea of continual motion, even if it isn't always forward movement, is part of the appeal of the metaphor.

every area of their lives—in their homes and families, at work, before the law. Activists in the first wave of the women's movement—the period extending from 1848, when the first women's rights convention occurred, to 1920, when women gained suffrage—did more than secure the vote for women. Because of the work of first wavers, by the end of the nineteenth century, a woman could hold property in her own name, even after marriage; she could keep the money she earned if she worked for pay; and she could enter into contracts as well as sue people. By 1920, a woman could go to college and earn higher degrees; she could enter the professions; and she could live on her own without the "protection" of a husband or male guardian. These rights may seem pretty basic to us today, but they had to be fought for. Similarly, women in the second wave in the 1960s and '70s agitated for and achieved many new rights for women, everything from greater access to employment and educational opportunities to reproductive rights, including abortion. Because of second wavers' activism, a girl can play sports on school and community teams, a pregnant woman can choose to have a certified midwife rather than an obstetrician deliver her child, and a woman who has been sexually assaulted can call a rape crisis hotline.

If women in the past have succeeded in making all of these gains, is there really any need for feminism today? Haven't women achieved equality already? While American women certainly have more rights today than ever before, they still have a long way to go. For one thing, they are not paid equally: These days a woman can expect to earn 77 cents to a man's dollar. Only twenty-three women are Fortune 500 CEOs; only 16.9 percent of the seats on corporate boards of directors are held by women. While there are more women involved in politics than ever, there are only twenty female U.S. senators (out of one hundred) and eighty-four female U.S. representatives (out of 435). Of the nine members of the Supreme Court, three are women, the largest number of women ever to serve at once. The social inequalities women face are as great as the economic and political ones. Women experience violence in their homes and families; they are subject to beauty ideals that encourage them to remake themselves through plastic surgery, skin bleaching, and disordered eating; and they have shrinking access to abortion, not to mention honest and thorough sex education. These continuing problems and inequalities suggest an ongoing need for feminist activism.

Feminism, however, is not just concerned with "equality." Many people take issue with the standard dictionary definition of feminism because it tends to reinforce an androcentric understanding of equality: Women will become equal when they have what men have. Should women want merely to copy men, though? Aren't there some flaws with the systems men have created? Indeed, aren't these flaws what feminist activists are trying to redress? Some scholars and activists talk about feminism in very different ways, shifting the focus away from women's trying to be like men and instead questioning whether women are even a unified category that can be understood to have the same interests and desires. In "Racism and Women's Studies," a talk delivered at the first National Women's Studies Association conference in 1979, writer and activist Barbara Smith offered the following definition of feminism; it is one of two that I prefer: "Feminism is the political theory and practice that struggles to free *all* women: women of color, working-class women, poor women, disabled women, Jewish women, lesbians, old women—as well as white, economically privileged, heterosexual women. Anything less than this vision of total freedom is not feminism, but merely female self-aggrandizement."

Perhaps the most striking thing about Smith's definition is its insistence that feminism is for *"all* women"; it is not a project or movement designed only for those with the privileges conferred by skin color, wealth, or sexual orientation. As Smith's definition insists, women come in all shapes and sizes, with all kinds of concerns; to talk about "women" as one broad category is thus impossible, since a black woman, for example, cannot separate her race and her sex—these axes of her identity intersect and are always present in her lived experience. She can never be just a black person; she can never be just a woman, either. According to Smith, then, feminism cannot be concerned solely with the oppression women face as women; it must be concerned with oppressions based on sex, race, class, ability, age, and sexual orientation, among other things. For instance, feminists are concerned about poor women's ability to find jobs and the social services they need; feminists work to assist lesbian mothers wanting to adopt children; and feminists question the ways the dominant culture depicts women of color in exotic, unrealistic, and demeaning ways.

Smith's definition does not use the word "equality"; instead, Smith states that feminism aims to "free *all* women." What might women need to be freed from? Smith's reference to freedom echoes the demands of activists in the civil rights and black power movements, not to mention the women's liberation movement of the 1960s and '70s; these radical feminists wanted to liberate women from the constraints and oppressions caused by patriarchy, a social system in which men rule and women are pushed into positions of inferiority and subservience. It is likely that for Smith, patriarchy was only one of many systems from which women needed liberation.

The definition of feminism offered by scholar bell hooks in *Feminist Theory: From Margin to Center,* the second definition that I prefer, helps to clarify other things from which women might need to be freed. hooks writes: "Feminism is a struggle to end sexist oppression. Therefore, it is necessarily a struggle to eradicate the ideology of domination that permeates Western culture on various levels, as well as a commitment to reorganizing society so that the self-development of people can take precedence over imperialism, economic expansion, and material desires."

This definition suggests that women need to be freed from sexism, or discrimination based on the belief that one sex is superior to the other. But hooks expands her critique so that it is not based just on sex; to hooks, "domination" is the root of the problem, and domination occurs when one person or group has power over another. According to hooks, society needs to be transformed so that all systems of domination, including not just patriarchy but racism, imperialism, and capitalism, are eradicated. All of society would be free if the "ideology of domination" were eliminated; as a result, people would be able to concentrate on "self-development." Feminism, then, can be thought of as a belief system that, by ending domination in all of its guises, liberates people so they can be their best selves. This liberation leads to social transformation.

Second wave feminists were not the first to conceptualize feminism in terms of liberation, however. The idea of liberation has been a recurring theme in the history of the women's movement. For instance, women's rights activists in the nineteenth century wanted to break free of the shackles of patriarchy and domesticity. They wanted the freedom to gain an education, to work for pay, and to lead in the church, and thus they wished to liberate themselves from confining and constraining social roles. One of the best examples, albeit fictional, of this desire for freedom from the nineteenth century's ideals of femininity is Edna Pontellier, the heroine of Kate Chopin's *The Awakening*. After beginning to awaken to sensuality during a summer vacation at the seaside, Edna returns home to New Orleans, where she abandons her duties as a conventional upper-middle-class matron, neglecting her work as hostess, homemaker, mother, and wife. Instead, she focuses on her own self-development, working on her painting, indulging her love for horse racing, amusing herself with a sexual dalliance, and even moving out of her husband's house when the desire to be independent overwhelms her. Near the end of the novel, Edna stands naked on the beach; divesting herself of her clothes is symbolic of the way she has attempted to rid herself of the constraints her society has imposed on her as a woman.

Like Edna, women in the second wave wanted to free themselves from social roles they saw as conventional and stifling; in seeking careers and sexual pleasure they hoped to find personal fulfillment in ways that had been unavailable to their mothers. These days, liberation takes other forms: Some women want to free themselves from body ideals that deny the female body's fullness and curves; other women seek freedom from patriarchal religious structures that do not give women any voice; still others wish to liberate themselves from the demand that women be able to "do it all," as if they were some kind of superhero.

While American women have been seeking liberation for hundreds of years, they did not always use the word "feminist" to refer to themselves or their goals. The word "feminism" was based on the French word *feminisme,* which was coined in the 1880s by Hubertine Auclert, the founder of the first woman suffrage society in France. The English started to use the word in the 1890s, and the term emerged in American publications somewhere around the turn of the century, coming into wide use in the 1910s. Before this time, women referred to their belief in "woman's rights," "woman suffrage," or the "woman movement," a broad term used to indicate women's works of benevolence and temperance as well as activism for higher education, better wages, and the vote. As Nancy Cott explains in *The Grounding of Modern Feminism,* even though to contemporary ears the phrase "woman movement" sounds strange and even grammatically incorrect, "Nineteenth-century women's consistent usage of the singular *woman* symbolized, in a word, the unity of the female sex. It proposed that all women have one cause, one movement." The phrase, then, worked as a call to solidarity, one that many women responded to during the course of the century. It is important to note, though, that the "woman movement" appealed only to those women who, because of their class and race privilege, were able to understand their identities in terms of their sex rather than in terms of any other identity category. Unlike Barbara Smith's "feminism," which is a movement for all women, the nineteenth-century "woman movement" was exclusive in its appeal to white, middle-class women.

By the time the term "feminism" came into widespread use in the 1910s, the idea of a "woman movement" sounded archaic, and the ideals of nineteenth-century womanhood themselves felt out of step with those held by more modern "New Women," who increasingly lived on their own in urban settings, had college educations, and worked in professional or semiprofessional jobs. The first users of the word "feminism" tended to capitalize the term and did not always specify what it meant. In 1914, suffragist Carrie Chapman Catt defined feminism as a "world-wide revolt against all artificial barriers which laws and customs interpose between women and human freedom." Catt, however, probably would not have called herself a "Feminist," since she saw suffrage as the most important goal that women's rights activists could achieve. In contrast, those who referred to themselves as "Feminists" saw the vote as essential and something to fight for, but they

Party Girls and Protofeminists

When we try to identify the moment when women ceased being restrained Victorian ladies concerned with propriety and convention, our minds often fasten onto the 1920s. During this decade, the "flapper" lived what seemed to be the high life; with her bobbed hair, short skirts, and playful attitude, the flapper seems to signal the advent of a freer woman, one whose liberated attitude toward sexuality mirrors that of our own age. However, it's important not to forget the flapper's precursor, the "New Woman," who became a type in the 1890s and remained popular until the advent of World War I.

The New Woman was young, well educated, and independent. She broke with convention in many ways, the most obvious being in her choice of dress. She typically wore a high-collared shirtwaist blouse, which she tucked into a dark skirt. This outfit underscored the New Woman's no-nonsense approach to life: Except for its puffed sleeves, the blouse was plain, and the skirt wasn't highly ornamented. It extended as far as her ankles, a length that made it easy to walk, hike, or ride a bicycle.

The most famous image of the New Woman was illustrator Charles Dana Gibson's "Gibson Girl." In countless images appearing in *Life* magazine in the 1890s, the Gibson Girl epitomized a new kind of American beauty, one that was self-confident, competent, and free. Although her long hair—worn piled onto her head—reflected an old-fashioned valuing of hair as women's "crowning glory," the New Woman's athleticism represented a new kind of physical freedom for women.

In *The New Womanhood*, a book published in 1904, author Winnifred Harper Cooley wrote, "The finest achievement of the new woman has been personal liberty. This is the foundation of civilization. . . . The new woman, in the sense of the best woman, the flower of all the womanhood of past ages, has come to stay—if civilization is to endure." Cooley suggested that the New Woman represented the pinnacle of womanhood; her "liberty," which set her apart from her Victorian predecessors, made her a model for early feminists in the period leading up to the First World War.

envisioned their goals more broadly, encompassing civil rights as well as opportunities for professional work, economic self-sufficiency, self-expression, and sexual freedom. As one woman stated, "All feminists are suffragists, but not all suffragists are feminists."

Although the term became more widespread in the 1910s, only a small group of women called themselves "feminists" in the early twentieth century; it wasn't until the late 1960s, when second wavers began to refer to themselves as feminists, that the term applied to a large constituency. Yet, even at first, some second wavers did not like the connotations of the word "feminist." To them, it called to mind, as activist Shulamith Firestone put it, a "granite-faced spinster obsessed with the vote." This association, of course, is ironic and anachronistic, but, in the minds of some radical women, a feminist was too white, too middle class, and too bourgeois in her desire for equality and her willingness to have women participate in "the system." Unlike these women, radical feminists such as Firestone wanted to make fundamental changes to society, rejecting a social system they saw as sexist and unfair to women. However, after doing some reading on early women's rights activists, Firestone, who would go on to publish the feminist classic *The Dialectic of Sex,* rethought her initial assessment of first wavers and criticized her peers who rejected any "connection with the old feminism, calling it kop-out [*sic*], reformist, bourgeois, without having bothered to examine the little . . . information there is on the subject." In coming to see that first wavers were more radical than she had initially judged them, Firestone helped to reclaim the word "feminist" and encourage her peers to apply it to themselves.

Firestone and her peers in the second wave articulated theories that have altered the way we talk about men, women, and society. Indeed, we can thank feminists for reshaping society's understanding of the roles, behaviors, and attitudes available to men and women. One of the key contributions of second wave feminists was the rejection of a traditional division of labor in which men were cast as breadwinners and women as homemakers. According to this norm, men's work took them into the public realm, where they were required to develop certain traits—competitiveness, strength, dominance—that would serve them well. In contrast, women were expected to remain in the private sphere and be the family's caregiver and domestic manager; for this role, women were encouraged to be dependent, nurturing, and cooperative. Feminists in the 1960s argued that these separate roles for women and men are not a product of nature or biology or God's will; instead, they are the result of social forces. Like the many theorists who have followed them, feminists distinguished between sex, or the biological and physiological distinctions between males and females, and gender, which refers to the social and cultural meanings ascribed to sexual differences. Feminist theorists in various disciplines talk about the way gender is socially constructed. Simply put, this means that gender is contingent on time, place, culture, and the interactions between people. For instance, being a female in 2016 means something quite different from what it meant in 1916 or 1816. Similarly, being a fifteen-year-old female in the United States today means something different from being the same age and sex in Iceland or Ghana or China. And even today within the United States, being female has different meanings depending on whether you are an African American girl living in rural California, a white girl growing up in an Illinois suburb, an Asian American in New York City, or an American Indian living on a reservation in South Dakota.

As second wave feminists developed theories about the social construction of gender, they realized that understanding women's status as separate from their biology meant that their status could be challenged and changed. Since girls didn't come into the world knowing how to cook, iron, sew, do laundry, or take care of children— they had to be taught these things—they could be taught different behaviors and traits and develop different aspirations. The same held true for boys. As a result of these beliefs, second wave feminists were particularly interested in gender socialization, the process whereby people learn the behaviors and attitudes that are considered appropriate for their sex. Because they recognized that children are socialized to "do gender" through the ways they are named, the toys they play with, and the TV shows and movies they watch, second wave feminists wanted to create alternatives so that children would be exposed to nonstereotypical representations of gender. Some feminists worked within their families so that husbands took on domestic responsibilities traditionally deemed "feminine," such as washing dishes, cooking, cleaning, and taking care of children. Others wrote children's books that challenged gender stereotypes, for instance by depicting a little boy who wants a doll. Contemporary feminists continue the work of questioning stereotypical gender roles and challenging the way children are socialized differently according to sex.

If feminism bequeathed one intellectual gift through its theorizing about the social construction of gender, it offered another in its conceptualization that "the personal is political." This phrase, which became a kind of mantra of the second wave, means that problems in women's everyday lives, problems such as domestic violence, access to contraception and abortion, quarrels with partners, challenges with parenting, and inequalities in the workplace, are not private concerns with private solutions. Instead, these seemingly personal and private issues have causes and consequences that are public and thus political; as a result, solutions to these problems can be found in the public arena and not solely with individuals who decide to change their behavior. One of the key ideas here is that power relations—"political" is used in this sense rather than to refer to electoral politics—affect women's personal relationships, their sex lives, their work lives. As Susan Douglas puts it, in claiming that "the personal is political," feminists meant that "motherhood, marriage, sexual behavior, and dress codes all had to be considered symptoms of a broader political and social system that kept women down."

When radical feminists in the 1960s and '70s began to talk with each other about their daily lives at work and at home, they realized that the unfair treatment they experienced from their bosses or their husbands' unwillingness to perform domestic chores were things they had in common. As they continued to discuss these issues, they discovered that they were not to blame for these problems; instead, social, cultural, and economic conditions created and reinforced them. After all, their bosses and husbands made assumptions about what women should do and what they as men should do, and these assumptions were the problem. In consciousness-raising groups, women sought to analyze and understand the attitudes and conditions that led to inequalities and then to do something to redress these inequalities. People no longer participate in consciousness-raising groups as such, although some people would argue that women's and gender studies classes offer a space where people can discuss and analyze personal problems in order to identify their public causes and consequences. Even if the phrase isn't used today as frequently as it was during the second wave, the insight that "the personal is political" has become such a part of our culture that people understand that the most private corners of their lives are shaped by power relations that are governed by society and culture.

The practice of consciousness-raising also revealed a commitment to the idea of sisterhood, the belief in women's working together as equals. In the first issue of *Ms.* magazine in 1972, its editor, Gloria Steinem, defined sisterhood as "deep personal connections of women . . . [which] often ignore barriers of age, economics, worldly experience, race, culture—all the barriers that, in male or mixed society, had seemed so difficult to cross." The idea of sisterhood had roots in the first wave of the women's movement. Although nineteenth-century women's rights activists would ultimately show allegiance principally to their white sisters, they manifested a kind of sisterhood in writing their women's rights treatise, the Declaration of Sentiments, which revealed their sympathy with women whose lives were very different from their own. The editors of *The History of Woman Suffrage* explain that the organizers of the first women's rights convention "had not in their own experience endured the coarser forms of tyranny resulting from unjust laws, or association with immoral and unscrupulous men, but they had souls large enough to feel the wrongs of others, without being scarified in their own flesh." Sisterhood, then, is about identifying with another person's lived experience; it demands a large "soul" with the capacity for empathy, "personal connection," and a commitment to working together. Above all, sisterhood elevates the importance of the collective over that of the individual. In both small groups and large organizations, feminists throughout history have been similarly motivated: Improving the lives of their "sisters," whether these were women exactly like them or not, was their highest priority.

Perhaps the biggest threat to sisterhood is competitive individualism, one of the beliefs on which our capitalistic American society is founded. This ideal privileges the well-being of the individual over that of the community or collective. A basic part of American culture, competitive individualism is what the American Dream is premised on: The idea is that, through hard work, a scrappy go-getter can claw her way to the top, gaining monetary rewards along the way. While the financial gains one acquires as a result of this ideal may be fulfilling to some, the costs are great: What is sacrificed is a sense of commitment to the greater good of the community.

© Fred W. McDarrah

Women marching up Fifth Avenue as part of the Women's Strike for Equality on August 26, 1970, which commemorated the fiftieth anniversary of women's suffrage.

Competitive individualism is, in some sense, a byproduct of feminism. That is, in gaining rights and opportunities for women, feminist activism has allowed women to be more self-sufficient and more able to concentrate on "self-development." Feminism has encouraged women to acquire not just civil rights but also the right to become individuals. While the development of a sense of individuality certainly corresponds to the "self-development" referred to by bell hooks, many people have taken the focus on the self to an extreme, which is not what hooks intended. Indeed, feminist successes have enabled many women to concentrate on their own interests rather than on those of a larger community. For instance, after the Nineteenth Amendment was ratified in 1920, masses of women shifted their attention away from feminist causes, and many simply concentrated on having a good time—after all, the "Roaring Twenties" was known for its party culture, and newly emancipated "flappers," with bobbed hair, shorter skirts, and greater economic and sexual freedom, were ready to take advantage of new cultural and social opportunities.

Similarly, we can see the 1980s, like the 1920s, as a decade that encouraged people to focus on themselves. After feminists in the 1960s and '70s struggled for, and gained, more opportunities for women, women in the '80s focused their attention on themselves: Many took high-powered jobs, put more attention into careers, and turned their attention away from causes that would benefit their "sisters." They looked instead at ways they could improve themselves, particularly in a physical sense. They spent money on cosmetics, gym memberships, and exercise equipment, all in a quest to be appealing to men and considered successful. As Susan Douglas writes in "Narcissism as Liberation," her chapter on advertisers' exploitation of feminist rhetoric in the 1980s, women were told to "forget the political already, and get back to the personal, which you might be able to do something about." One of the goals of feminism, then, is to remind women that if their focus is exclusively on themselves, much is lost: In addition to change that could be accomplished on behalf of oppressed groups,

What Is Feminism, Anyway?

"I myself have never been able to find out precisely what feminism is: I only know that people call me a feminist whenever I express sentiments that differentiate me from a doormat."

—Rebecca West, *The Clarion*, 1913

"My definition of feminism is simply that women are people, in the fullest sense of the word, who must be free to move in society with all the privileges and opportunities and responsibilities that are their human and American right."

—Betty Friedan, *It Changed My Life:
Writings on the Women's Movement*, 1976

"I am a feminist, and what that means to me is much the same as the meaning of the fact that I am Black: it means that I must undertake to love myself and to respect myself as though my very life depends upon self-love and self-respect."

—June Jordan, *Civil Wars*, 1981

"Third World feminism is about feeding people in all their hungers."

—Cherríe Moraga, *Loving in the War Years*, 1983

competitive individualists lose out on a sense of commitment to something larger than themselves.

There's another aspect of the definition of feminism that I haven't discussed yet, and it has to do with the second part of the dictionary definition, which states that feminism is a "movement organized around [the] belief" in the equality of the sexes. Used in this sense, "movement" generally implies a large-scale organized effort to do something. While it is certainly important to read and learn about the history of the feminist movement—the rest of this book will trace out the history of the first, second, and third waves of feminism—the language of "movements" can be confusing and even off-putting. It can

"Feminism's agenda is basic: It asks that women not be forced to 'choose' between public justice and private happiness. It asks that women be free to define themselves—instead of having their identity defined for them, time and again, by their culture and their men."

—Susan Faludi, *Backlash: The Undeclared War Against American Women,* 1991

"[F]eminism is no longer a group of organizations or leaders. . . . It's the way we talk about and treat one another. It's who makes the money and who makes the compromises and who makes the dinner. It's a state of mind. It's the way we live now."

—Anna Quindlen, *New York Times,* 1994

"What [feminism] means to me is that you don't let your gender define who you are—you can be who you want to be. If everyone has a fair chance to be what they want to be and do what they want to do, it's better for everyone."

—Joseph Gordon-Levitt, 2014

"Feminism is the radical notion that women are people."

—Bumper sticker

seem to imply a unified type of action, and the women's movement, as the following chapters indicate, has rarely been unified. Indeed, feminism has thrived on contention and difference; the fact that there are so many different definitions of "feminism" suggests that feminists have various ideas about the goals of their work. Just as a group of Democrats has different opinions about social, political, and economic issues, a group of feminists believes multiple things about the goals of feminism. Just as there is no one feminism, there is no one feminist movement.

In the introduction to the 1970 anthology *Sisterhood Is Powerful,* radical feminist Robin Morgan writes:

This is a not a movement one "joins." There are no rigid structures or membership cards. The Women's Liberation Movement exists where three or four friends or neighbors decide to meet regularly over coffee and talk about their personal lives. It also exists in the cells of women's jails, on the welfare lines, in the supermarket, the factory, the convent, the farm, the maternity ward, the street corner, the old ladies' home, the kitchen, the steno pool, the bed. It exists in your mind and in the political and personal insights that you can contribute to change and shape and help its growth.

Although it is describing feminism of the late 1960s and early '70s, this passage has relevance for feminism throughout American history. While certainly there have been brief periods when there has been a recognizable women's "movement" that one could be part of, for much of the last 165 years, women have worked informally—both individually and collectively—to secure rights for women. Feminist organizations certainly do exist, but, as Morgan asserts, feminism is most essentially a way of thinking and of acting in the world. By transforming our understanding of power relations in men and women's lives, feminism can teach us how to transform society itself so that both equality and liberation can be achieved.

CHAPTER 2

First Wave Feminism: Fighting for the Vote

IMAGINE THAT YOU ARE A WHITE, middle-class woman living in the United States two hundred years ago, well before members of the first wave of the women's movement started agitating for women's rights. What would your life have been like?

For starters, you would have had a limited education, more than likely attending school for only a handful of years. At school, you would have learned to read, write, and do arithmetic; you would also have studied needlework and other domestic arts since one of the purposes of education for your sex was to teach you to be a good homemaker. Unless you attended an exclusive northeastern seminary, such as those run by Sarah Pierce, Emma Willard, Catharine Beecher, or Mary Lyon, you would not have studied subjects such as history, geography, classics, French, mathematics, or the natural or physical sciences. If you were lucky enough to attend such an academy, your schooling would have ended once you graduated; no colleges were open to females until Oberlin admitted women in 1837.

If you desired more education, you were viewed with suspicion and called a "bluestocking," a derisive term for an intellectual woman who wanted freedoms beyond those her role as wife and mother permitted her. Brainy women faced ostracism because, according to prevailing beliefs, their intellectual efforts sapped them of the energy their uteruses would need to function. Proper women were expected to adhere to the four tenets of what the historian Barbara Welter has referred to as the "cult of true womanhood": piety, purity, domesticity, and submissiveness. According to this code of conduct, your virtue was measured in terms of your religious devotion, your sexual purity, your excellence as a homemaker, and your willingness to defer to the men in your life. If you deviated from the norms of this cult of domesticity, you were considered an outcast.

Although you were deemed more spiritual than your fathers, husbands, and brothers, your sex made you ineligible not just for the ministry but for virtually all public work in the church. You were expected to live a quiet, domestic life away from the corrupting influence of the public realm. Indeed, since your education was minimal, you would not be able to find much lucrative work in any field, and careers not just in ministry but in medicine, law, and business would be closed to you. If your husband died and you did need to earn money, you might be able to find low-paying work as a teacher, housekeeper, or seamstress.

Once you were married, you would lose your legal identity, as you gave up your "maiden" name to become Mrs. John Doe. Under what is referred to as coverture, your civil identity would vanish, and you would no longer be able to own property, including any wages you earned. You would not be able to sue or to enter into contracts, either. If you were a single woman, you had more legal rights than a married one, but society looked down on unattached women, scorning them as "spinsters."

After your marriage, you would relinquish your virginity, formerly your most prized possession, and your body would no longer belong to you. You would be expected to respond to your husband's sexual desires; you were thought to have no sexual appetites of your own. Because reliable birth control did not exist, you would be pregnant often: The average woman in 1800 had around seven children.

As a married woman, you would be expected to submit to your husband's rules, obeying his commands and accepting his punishments. Even if your husband beat you, it would be extremely difficult to secure a divorce; if you were lucky enough to end an abusive marriage, very likely your husband would gain custody of your children.

And if you disagreed with any of the preceding customs and rules, you wouldn't be able to do much to change them since you would not be able to vote. As a result of having no representation in the legislature, you would have to obey laws whose creators you had no role in electing.

If you were a white woman of lesser economic means, you were expected to work, and the ideals of the cult of domesticity had less applicability to you. If you lived on a farm, for instance, you spent most of your waking hours performing outdoor tasks, such as working in vegetable gardens, tending dairies, and caring for poultry, and completing endless domestic chores, such as spinning, weaving, and sewing; making butter and cheese; and salting, smoking, and drying meat. Because such work usually led only to subsistence, not income, when textile factories sprang up in towns such as Lowell, Massachusetts, they attracted you away from the farm with the promise of earning money to send back to your cash-poor family.

If you were a working-class white woman living in one of the growing cities on the East Coast, you had few ways to earn money. If you were married, you might take in lodgers to make ends meet. If you were a single woman, you might enter domestic service; many Irish women followed this route when they immigrated to the United States. If you were a free woman of color, you had few other employment opportunities besides domestic labor.

If you were a female member of a matrilineal Indian tribe—and approximately two-thirds of Native American tribes were—the work you did, and not the virtues you displayed, gained you respect in your community. In charge of food production, you made decisions about planting, harvesting, and food processing; because your culture was matrilocal, you lived with your parents' family after you married. Yet, your status in this female-centered society was to be short-lived: As disease decimated indigenous populations and as remaining native peoples moved away from the eastern seaboard, fewer and fewer Native American women survived to experience such equality.

While opportunities were constrained for white and indigenous women, things were markedly worse for their black sisters. If you were a black woman in the early nineteenth century, chances are you were a slave. As a slave, you were not educated since you were valued principally as a body that performed manual labor and produced offspring. In fact, in many places, the law forbade teaching slaves to read. Also illegal were slave marriages: Even if male and female slaves joined together in matrimony, the law did not recognize these unions, and slave owners could—and did—separate wives from their husbands and children when estates were sold and property was dispersed.

Although some white people sympathized with your condition as a slave, to many whites, you did not qualify as a "true" woman because of your alleged lack of sexual purity. If your white master impregnated you, the stigma of illegitimacy adhered not to him but to you; as a black woman, you were seen as sexually available and promiscuous.

Although we might expect all women to chafe against such limited opportunities, many white, middle-class women felt empowered through their rule in their homes; many gained status as arbiters of their family's piety, morality, and purity and earned their loved ones' respect through their skills as nurses and domestic managers. Others felt that, because women did not participate in the "dirty" world of commerce that was taking hold in the early nineteenth century, they were morally and spiritually elevated, even exalted.

Yet, some people—usually women with advanced education and sometimes with economic and social privilege—did question women's status in society. One such person was Englishwoman Mary Wollstonecraft, whose *Vindication of the Rights of Woman* was published in 1792. A witness to the French Revolution and a believer in Enlightenment ideals such as democracy and the rights of man, Wollstonecraft questioned not just the tyranny of monarchy but men's tyranny within the family, desiring women to have power over themselves. In her *Vindication,* Wollstonecraft urged her white, middle-class readers, both male and female, to provide identical educations for boys and girls. Wollstonecraft blamed women's lack of social status on their inferior schooling; instead of being educated to be the equals of men, women were taught to use their beauty and feminine charms to entrap men in marriage. In contrast, Wollstonecraft believed that women should learn how to support themselves. Although Wollstonecraft suggested that women might "be physicians as well as nurses" or "study politics," her principal aim was to correct an educational system that created a class of frivolous women. Perhaps as much as anything else, she wanted to see women trained to be responsible mothers and thoughtful wives. Although some freethinking men and women admired her views, the public attacked Wollstonecraft for her radical ideas, referring to her as a "hyena in petticoats."

Women such as Wollstonecraft and the American transcendentalist Margaret Fuller, whose *Woman in the Nineteenth Century* (1844) also advocated women's access to education and jobs, used their writing to convince the public of the constrained social roles available to women. Other women, however, took a different approach, working to reform social institutions through organized activist work. As a result of the Second Great Awakening in the early nineteenth century, white, middle-class women began to gain more public acceptance in the church. Because this religious movement emphasized emotional conversion experiences as opposed to the doctrine promoted by highly educated ministers, women gained power in churches and decided to act on their moral feelings by creating benevolent and missionary societies that would help the poor. Some women moved from benevolent organizations to temperance and antislavery work. This was particularly true of the women who were involved in the abolition movement, who, fueled by their religious beliefs, saw their work as a way to save the souls of white slave owners and their black slaves. Because of their sex and their roles as mothers, female members of the antislavery movement also felt great sympathy with black female slaves, whose lives were frequently violated by the white men who raped them and separated them from their husbands and children.

However, in spite of their passionate commitment to the cause, women were typically excluded from antislavery groups; as a result, they formed associations of their own, such as the Boston Female Anti-Slavery Society and the Philadelphia Female Anti-Slavery Society. Doubly excluded were free black women, who were generally barred from groups run by both

Outlawing "Demon Rum"

Even before they got involved in the antislavery movement, many women's rights activists fought for temperance, the movement to outlaw the sale of alcohol. It seemed like a natural cause for women—after all, under the influence of alcohol, men could squander an entire paycheck and, worse, physically abuse their wives and children. It was thus certainly in the interest of women to limit men's access to intoxicating spirits. The women who did temperance work were usually white; some were middle class, while others were poor or working class.

Although people had been working for liquor reform since the 1820s, women became more involved in the temperance movement in the 1870s, when an evangelical "crusade" against alcohol emerged in the Midwest and caught on in towns and villages throughout the country. Women banded together, marched to local taverns, and knelt down in prayer, asking saloon owners to close their doors. Perhaps the most famous of these crusaders was Carrie Nation, who used her imposing stature—she was reportedly six feet tall—to her advantage, bursting into bars and smashing windows, mirrors, and liquor bottles to communicate her distaste for "demon rum."

While barkeepers often complied with the crusaders' requests, saloons quickly reopened, and women wanted a more permanent organization devoted to temperance. To fill this need, the Woman's Christian Temperance Union (WCTU) was organized in 1874, with Annie Wittenmyer as

white women and black men; in response, black women created their own antislavery organizations, such as the Manhattan Abolition Society and the Colored Female Anti-Slavery Society. From all of these groups, black and white women learned a great deal about activism: They developed strategies for organizing, they learned to persuade people about the righteousness of their cause, they asked people to sign petitions, and they raised funds. They also learned more about women's unequal social status than they might have expected to.

The experience of the Grimké sisters illustrates the convergence of activism on behalf of slaves and women. Born into a prominent slaveholding family from South Carolina, Sarah Grimké and her its president and Frances Willard as its corresponding secretary. Willard, who led the organization from the late 1870s to the late 1890s, had a particular genius for involving women in all kinds of activism; by establishing "departments" in the WCTU, she created a way for women to perform everything from educational and prison reform to public health and suffrage work. In this way, women who ordinarily would not have been suffrage workers became part of the movement. As the largest women's organization in the nation, the WCTU did a great deal to teach women about the need for a voice in public affairs.

In spite of Willard's organizational talents, the WCTU, like many women's groups of the time, excluded people whose ethnic or religious affiliations were judged as suspect. Members of the WCTU often manifested nativist views, critiquing first Irish and German immigrants and later southern and eastern European ones, people whose cultural and religious backgrounds accepted alcohol consumption. When African Americans and immigrants joined the WCTU, they tended to affiliate with separate branches designated for people of their racial and ethnic groups.

Although many women became part of the suffrage campaign as a result of the WCTU, some women's rights activists were hesitant to welcome temperance reformers, who had created much antagonism among liquor companies. Suffragists were worried that their cause would be linked with temperance and that men who might have considered enfranchising women would oppose the idea if they believed that women would vote for prohibition.

younger sister, Angelina, struggled to reconcile their Christian faith with their family's ownership of slaves. Believers from an early age in the immorality of the South's "peculiar institution," the sisters ultimately joined the Society of Friends in Charleston before moving to Philadelphia in the 1820s. In their new home, the sisters became actively involved in the antislavery movement after a letter Angelina sent to the abolitionist William Lloyd Garrison appeared in his newspaper, *The Liberator*. Because of the public's enthusiastic response to this letter and because of the sisters' potential value to the abolition movement as firsthand witnesses to slavery, the American Anti-Slavery Society brought the Grimkés to New York to speak in early 1837. By lecturing in public, the Grimké sisters violated an unspoken rule of the cult of domesticity: Respectable women did not exit the private sphere of the home to put themselves forward and speak out in mixed company. The reaction to the Grimkés was hostile; the press referred to Angelina as "Devileena," and the prominent educator Catharine Beecher criticized the sisters for indecorous behavior. Perhaps most seriously, the Council of Congregationalist Ministers of Massachusetts issued a pastoral letter condemning the Grimkés, stating: "The power of woman is her dependence. . . . But when she assumes the place and tone of man as a public reformer . . . she yields the power which God has given her for her protection, and her character becomes unnatural." Such reactions enabled the Grimkés to see the connection between the oppression of slaves and women. Sarah Grimké developed her ideas on women's rights in her *Letters on the Equality of the Sexes,* published in 1838; challenging the idea of female inferiority and dependence, Grimké used the Bible to assert the equality of men and women. She wrote: "I ask no favors for my sex. . . . All I ask our brethren is, that they will take their feet from off our necks and permit us to stand upright on that ground which God designed us to occupy."

The Grimké sisters did not have a long activist career: After marrying the abolitionist Theodore Weld in 1838, Angelina raised a family with help from Sarah, who came to live with the Weld family. But other women in the abolitionist movement echoed their critique of the treatment of women. One such woman, Emily Collins, remembered: "All through the Anti-Slavery struggle, every word of denunciation of the wrongs of the Southern slave, was, I felt, equally applicable to the wrongs of my own sex. Every argument for the emancipation of the colored man, was equally one for that of woman; and I was surprised that all Abolitionists did not see the similarity in the condition of the two classes." In their *History of Woman Suffrage,* Elizabeth Cady Stanton and Susan B. Anthony asserted that "above all other causes of the 'Woman Suffrage Movement' was the Anti-Slavery Struggle. . . . In the early Anti-Slavery conventions, the broad principles of human rights were so exhaustively discussed, justice, liberty, and equality, so clearly taught, that the women who crowded to listen, readily learned the lesson of freedom for themselves, and early began to take part in the debates and business affairs of all associations."

By midcentury it even became somewhat more common for women to speak in public. The work of abolition prepared future women's rights activists for agitating for an unpopular cause, one that would not be received well by the majority. Unlike more mainstream temperance reform, which also gave women experience in activism, antislavery work readied women for the hostile reactions of a public unprepared for a new way of thinking about women and their rights.

Traditionally recognized as the beginning of the organized women's movement in the United States, the Seneca Falls Convention of July 1848 was put together on the spur of the moment by a handful of dedicated women. When Lucretia Mott, a Quaker minister and antislavery activist, and Elizabeth Cady Stanton, a young woman twenty-two years her junior, renewed their friendship in upstate New York, the two women decided to fulfill a goal they had set eight years before at the World Anti-Slavery Society convention in London, where they had met. Both active in the abolition movement, Mott and Stanton were outraged at the decision of the convention's organizers not to allow elected female delegates to sit with their male peers. This exclusion rankled; it clearly revealed women's marginal status within the antislavery movement. An elected delegate, Mott watched the conference proceedings with Stanton from an upstairs gallery; together they decided to redress the wrongs of women at a future convention, which they would lead.

Although eight years intervened before such a conference occurred, when the two women met again in the summer of 1848 they found their desire for a meeting on "the social, civil, and religious rights of woman" had not diminished. With the help of three other women, Jane Hunt, Martha Wright, and Mary Ann McClintock, Mott and Stanton organized the conference in less than a week, finding a suitable location in a nearby chapel and announcing the event in an area newspaper. To give the meeting a focus, Stanton drafted a Declaration of Sentiments, which articulated the wrongs done to women. Using the Declaration of Independence as a rhetorical model, Stanton's document announced women's equality with men and outlined the grievances women had with their treatment in American society. Chief among these grievances were women's inability to vote, their consequent lack of representation in government, and their invisibility before the law. To accompany the Declaration of Sentiments, Stanton wrote a set of resolutions, which provided matter for debate and discussion at the convention. Although the three hundred attendees—among them, forty men—agreed on resolutions pertaining to women's exclusion from higher education, the professions, and the ministry as well as married women's constrained legal status under coverture, the resolution demanding woman suffrage, as it was referred to in the nineteenth century, proved to be divisive. Stanton and the abolitionist Frederick Douglass argued in favor of suffrage, and they ultimately convinced the conference's attendees of its importance in securing many of the other resolutions.

The majority's discomfort with the idea of woman suffrage at the first women's rights convention indicates Stanton's status as a revolutionary, but it also foreshadows that suffrage would not be the main issue discussed at the antebellum women's rights conferences that were held virtually every year between 1850 and 1860; indeed, these meetings had multifaceted agendas, promoting suffrage along with a host of other reforms, including property rights and greater access to education and employment for women. As this list of goals would suggest, those who sought rights for women typically envisioned the concerns of white, middle-class, married women. For instance, the Married Women's Property Act, which Stanton and social activists Ernestine Rose and Paulina Wright Davis lobbied for in the 1840s and which passed the New York State legislature in 1848, secured ownership only of the property that married women had had before their marriages and inherited afterward; it did not allow women to keep the wages they earned during marriage.

Just as the class affiliation of early women's rights activists limited their point of view, so did their racial attitudes. When the former slave

Radical Rags

Bloomers: It's hard to believe that a word we associate now with under-garments would have anything to do with the nineteenth-century women's movement, but it does. In fact, one of the most practical undertakings by women's rights activists in the midnineteenth century was to seek to change women's clothing. Women at the time wore corsets, petticoats, and long dresses, all of which constrained their movement. Stiff corsets, often made of bone, gave women the wasp waists then in vogue but often led to breathing difficulties, poor digestion, and, most seriously, the per-manent shifting of internal organs. As Elizabeth Smith Miller, the creator of a new costume for women, stated, "Working in my garden—weeding & transplanting in bedraggled skirts that clung in fettered folds about my feet & ankles, I became desperate and resolved on immediate release."

In late 1850, Miller's costume—a loose, "short" skirt extending four inches below the knees that was worn over ballooning, "Turkish" trou-sers—caught on among such women's rights activists as Miller's cousin Elizabeth Cady Stanton and the latter's friend, Amelia Bloomer, the pub-lisher of a temperance newspaper called *The Lily*. Because Bloomer pro-moted the new style of dress in her paper, writing about it and printing pictures and patterns, people started to refer to the new mode of dress as "bloomerettes," the "bloomer costume," and finally "bloomers."

As strange as it may seem to us now, some women's rights activists be-lieved that a change in their style of dress could give women more status in society. Gerrit Smith, Miller's father and Stanton's cousin, stated that by donning more practical clothing, women could ensure that men would no longer treat them like "playthings, idols, or dolls." Smith was more ready for sartorial change than most other men—or women, for that matter; those who wore "bloomers" during their heyday in the early 1850s were roundly derided. Most people thought that the new costume was indecent since it showed the outline of women's legs. Stanton wore bloomers for several years but returned to long dresses in 1854, convinced that the "mental bondage" caused by public ostracism far outweighed the "physi-cal freedom" afforded by the new clothing style. She convinced other ac-tivists to return to conventional attire so that the public would concentrate on their ideas and message rather than their clothes and appearance.

Sojourner Truth spoke at a women's rights convention in Akron, Ohio, in 1851, she was met with great hostility from an audience of allegedly enlightened white people. Truth was at the convention to sell her recently published autobiography, *The Narrative of Sojourner Truth: A Northern Slave*. Truth's life certainly warranted a retelling: Born around 1797 in the Hudson River Valley of New York, Truth was the daughter of Dutch-speaking parents, who named her Isabella. After gaining freedom in 1827, when slavery was abolished in New York, Truth underwent a religious conversion when Jesus appeared to her in a vision; she began to attend a Methodist church, first in Kingston, New York, and later in New York City, where she moved in 1829. In New York, Truth started to preach at camp meetings, joined a commune, and worked as a domestic servant and laundress. Although religion was central to her life, it wasn't until 1843, when God commanded her to leave the city and rename herself, that Truth became an itinerant evangelist. During her travels, Truth met abolitionists and started to speak at antislavery meetings more than she did at religious revivals. In fact, she became such a popular speaker that she joined the antislavery circuit in the late 1840s.

As a result of her connection with abolition, the people present at the Akron conference were worried that Truth would speak out against slavery and thus detract from the event's focus on women's rights; to show their disapproval, the audience verbally harassed her when she moved to the podium to speak. Not to be silenced, Truth spoke eloquently about her condition as a woman to a gathered crowd who, like society at large, saw her in terms of her race instead of her sex. Truth demanded to be acknowledged for who she was: a black woman who, because of her color, was never treated with delicacy or deference. As she stated,

That man over there says that women need to be helped into carriages and lifted over ditches, and to have the best place everywhere. Nobody ever helps me into carriages or over mud puddles, or gives me any best place. And ain't I a woman? Look at me! I have ploughed and planted and gathered into barns and no man could head me. And ain't I a woman?

I could work as much and eat as much as a man—when I
could get it—and bear the lash as well. And ain't I a woman?
I have borne thirteen children and seen most all sold off to
slavery, and when I cried out with my mother's grief, none
but Jesus heard me. And ain't I a woman?

After insisting on her importance in spite of her despised status, Truth matched wits with the male clerics who had already spoken at the conference, outlining biblical arguments for women's inferiority. By refuting their reasoning, she gained the respect of the assembled crowd. In her recollection of the event, Frances Dana Gage, the presiding member of the conference, wrote that Truth "had taken us up in her strong arms and carried us safely over the slough of difficulty, turning the whole tide in our favor. I have never in my life seen anything like the magical influence that subdued the snobbish spirit of the day and turned the sneers and jeers of an excited crowd into notes of respect and admiration."

As a charismatic, larger-than-life figure, Sojourner Truth grew to be recognized, symbolically at least, as the nineteenth century's most prominent black women's rights leader. However, other black women were involved in activism in the antebellum period, although most of these women focused their work on abolition as opposed to women's rights. Most of these women were free middle-class black women from the North. For example, when men excluded women from Philadelphia's American Anti-Slavery Society, the African American women Charlotte, Margaretta, and Sarah Forten and Sarah and Grace Douglass joined with Lucretia Mott to create a female abolitionist group. Another black female activist was Frances Ellen Watkins Harper. The daughter of free blacks, Harper grew up in Baltimore and worked as a teacher in Pennsylvania and Ohio, where

Library of Congress

Sojourner Truth, photographed in Detroit in 1864.

she became involved with the Underground Railroad. Harper's public work on behalf of abolition took several forms: working in antislavery societies, delivering speeches, and writing poetry about the cruelties of slavery. Harriet Jacobs also chronicled the brutality of slavery; in *Incidents in the Life of a Slave Girl,* her autobiographical account of her years in servitude, Jacobs openly discussed the sexual exploitation and abuse she and other slave women experienced. Although her book's publication coincided with the start of the Civil War, Jacobs worked to abolish slavery and to help slave refugees during the war.

The 1850s marked a fruitful period in women's rights activism, mainly because of the activity and leadership of three women: Elizabeth Cady Stanton, Susan B. Anthony, and Lucy Stone. Stanton had long felt outraged by the injustices done to her sex. Born in 1815 to a wealthy and well-connected family in upstate New York, Stanton was educated at local schools and attended Emma Willard's Troy Female Seminary in the early 1830s. Perhaps just as important as her formal education was the time she spent in the offices of her father, a judge; there, she read his law books and heard his counsel to the many people who came to see him. In particular, she remembered one occasion when her father could do nothing to help a woman whose husband had squandered her inheritance; she had no legal recourse because the law did not protect wives against the profligate behavior of their husbands. Witnessing her father's inability to help this woman convinced the young Stanton of the need to change unjust laws that could ruin women's lives.

In spite of her passionate belief in the need for reform of women's inferior legal status, in many ways Stanton conformed to the cult of domesticity. In 1840, she married the abolitionist speaker Henry Stanton, whose reforming zeal did not fully extend to the struggle for women's rights. When they married, the couple struck the word "obey" from their wedding vows, thinking of their union as one of equals. Flouting convention, Stanton wished to be referred to as Mrs. Elizabeth Cady Stanton, instead of the more usual Mrs. Henry Stanton. Yet, after Stanton read her husband a draft of the Declaration of Sentiments and Resolutions, he not only stated his disapproval of the resolution that demanded women's suffrage but also left town to emphasize his opinion. In some ways, Stanton lived a life that resembled those of many wives and mothers at midcentury. Although she spent the early years of her marriage in Boston, where she had a circle of activist friends and attended lectures on the intellectual and reform topics she cared deeply about, her life changed in 1847 when her husband opened a law practice in Seneca Falls, New York. In this rural town and amid the responsibilities of her ever-growing family—she would ultimately have seven children—Stanton felt isolated and overwhelmed by her life of domestic drudgery. Her friendship with Susan B. Anthony, which facilitated her involvement in the women's rights movement, saved her from isolation and unhappiness.

Although her name may be more familiar than Stanton's, Susan B. Anthony was something of a latecomer to women's rights, focusing her early activist energies on the causes of abolition and temperance. Born in rural Massachusetts in 1820 to reform-loving parents, Anthony was educated locally and at a Quaker boarding school in Philadelphia. When her father went bankrupt in 1837, she was forced to leave school and seek employment as a teacher, a job at which she worked for more than ten years before moving to Rochester, New York, where her family had settled in the 1840s. Although her parents and younger sister told her about Elizabeth Cady Stanton after attending a women's rights meeting in 1848, Anthony was initially reluctant to introduce herself to Stanton and become involved in such activism; her interest at this time was in temperance work. However, when Anthony met Stanton after an antislavery lecture in 1851, a deep friendship was born. In fact, for the next fifty years, Anthony and Stanton were nearly inseparable, working together for temperance, women's rights, and, above all, suffrage.

Perhaps one factor in the long duration of the two women's friendship, apart from their like-minded thinking, was their complementary personalities and lives. On the surface, the two women could hardly have been more different: At this time the mother of several rambunctious boys, the ebullient Stanton was lively and talkative, while the unmarried Anthony was reserved, self-conscious, and serious.

In spite of these differences, the women worked together extremely well. While Stanton's many children and domestic duties inhibited her ability to travel, Anthony's singleness meant she could visit Stanton and go on extended speaking tours. In many ways, Anthony provided Stanton with the intellectual companionship and contact with the outside world that she craved while she was largely homebound in Seneca Falls. The following description indicates Stanton's fondness for her collaborator: "[W]henever I saw that stately Quaker girl coming across my lawn, I knew that some happy convocation of the sons of Adam were to be set by the ears, by one of our appeals or resolutions. The little portmanteau stuffed with facts was opened. . . . Then we would get out our pens and write articles for papers, or a petition to the Legislature, letters to the faithful. . . . We never met without issuing a pronunciamento on some question. . . ."

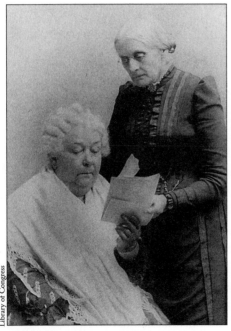

Library of Congress

Elizabeth Cady Stanton and Susan B. Anthony worked tirelessly for women's suffrage.

Whereas Stanton was a great and fluent writer and thinker, Anthony felt clumsy as an author, leaving much of her speech writing to her older friend. Anthony, however, had considerable talents of her own: She was an excellent manager, organizer, and strategist, and her single-minded dedication to the cause of suffrage often served to check Stanton's impulsive tendency to involve herself in a multitude of women's issues. Stanton explained the friends' collaboration as follows: "In writing we did better work together than either could alone. While she is slow and analytical in composition, I am rapid and synthetic. I am the better writer, she the better critic. She supplied the facts and statistics, I the philosophy and rhetoric, and together we have made arguments that have stood unshaken by the storms of thirty long years."

Lucy Stone's background was more humble than either Stanton's or Anthony's. Born in western Massachusetts in 1818, Stone grew up on her family's farm. She had a difficult relationship with her father, who personified the parsimonious, withdrawn New Englander of the early nineteenth century. As Stone recalled, "There was only one will in our home, and that was my father's." Unlike Anthony, who was reared in a gentle and loving Quaker family, Stone experienced the repressive piety of her Congregationalist parents, who repeatedly reminded their children of the perils of eternal damnation. A sensitive child who reacted against the literal biblical teachings of her parents' religion, Stone refused to see women's subordination as divinely ordained. The remedy she sought was higher education: Stone wanted to go to college. Convincing her father to let her attend school until she could teach to support herself—at this time, schoolteachers merely had to demonstrate proficiency at reading, writing, and arithmetic but didn't need any advanced training—Stone borrowed money from him to pay for her early education. For nine years, she worked as a teacher, saving money to attend high school and later one term at Oberlin College, where she paid her way by working as a housekeeper, laundress, and teacher. After she completed her degree, Stone began to work as a public speaker for the Anti-Slavery Society of Massachusetts, which soon reprimanded her for spending as much time outlining the plight of women as she did the error of slavery. Stone solved this ostensible conflict of interest by doing her antislavery lecturing on weekends and speaking about "the elevation of my sex" during the week. By all accounts, Stone was a gifted orator; even as she encountered the jeers of hostile crowds, she spoke out passionately but composedly in a melodious, penetrating voice. Although Stone ultimately married, her partnership with the reformer Henry Blackwell did not detract from her women's rights work. Her radical decision to keep her own name after her marriage led to the usage, even into the twentieth century, of the phrase "Lucy Stoner" to refer to a woman who made a similar choice.

Although Stanton, Anthony, Stone, and a host of other committed women worked diligently for women's rights in the twenty years after the Seneca Falls convention, the movement remained decentralized, having instead of a permanent organization a steering committee made up of women from states with active campaigns. Because of the treatment many reformers had received within the hierarchical and sexist antislavery organizations, women's rights activists remained skeptical of central organizations until after the Civil War. Until then, they communicated their ideas not just through local conventions but through the mainstream press when they could get its attention, the abolitionist newspapers, and journals that they created and edited. Among the most prominent of these publications dedicated to transmitting information about women's rights were Jane Swisshelm's *Pittsburgh Saturday Visiter,* a newspaper begun in 1847 that explored temperance, abolition, and women's rights; Amelia Bloomer's *The Lily,* a newspaper started in 1849 that focused on temperance; and Paulina Wright Davis's *The Una,* a newspaper launched in 1853 that covered "the rights, sphere, duty, and destiny of woman, fully and fearlessly."

Although women's rights activism was gaining momentum in the 1850s—for instance, because of the work of Stanton, Anthony, and others, New York state passed a revised Married Women's Property Act in 1860, giving women joint custody of their children and allowing them to keep their wages, make wills, and inherit property—the onset of the Civil War interrupted this work. Women committed themselves to war work through organizations such as the Sanitary Commission and abandoned their crusade for women's rights, believing that the time was not right for such activism. Stanton and Anthony did not make the transition to war work easily; at the start of the war, they were at a loss for what to do until Stanton's husband suggested that they work to get signatures in support of a constitutional amendment to end slavery. In 1863, they formed the Women's National Loyal League;

in the course of fifteen months, they succeeded in getting four hundred thousand signatures, thereby showing Congress the public's support of a measure to ban slavery. In undertaking and completing this work, Stanton, Anthony, and other women's rights activists thought that, at the end of the war, they would be rewarded with suffrage. Although such a view may now seem naive, they believed that, because their former abolitionist allies had close ties with the ruling Republican Party, these men would be in a position to reward all women for their service to the Union. What ended up happening, however, was a far cry from what they anticipated; instead, arguments over the citizenship and suffrage of freed black slaves led to a division in the women's rights community.

At the end of the war, abolitionists and women's rights activists formed the American Equal Rights Association (AERA), whose goal was to gain civil rights for both black people and women. However, when Congress began to discuss the Fourteenth Amendment in 1866, it became clear to women's rights activists that it would protect only the rights of men; for the first time in the Constitution, there would be a reference to "male" citizens. Instead of allying themselves with Lucy Stone, Henry Blackwell, and the abolitionists who were the core members of the AERA, activists such as Stanton and Anthony challenged the exclusivity of the Fourteenth Amendment, seeking signatures to a petition that would halt the amendment's progress. Indeed, Anthony stated, "I will cut off this right arm of mine before I will ever work for or demand the ballot for the Negro and not the woman." In spite of their work against it, the Fourteenth Amendment was ratified in 1868; six months later, Republicans introduced the Fifteenth Amendment, which stated, "The right of citizens of the United States to vote shall not be denied or abridged by the United States or by any State, on account of race, color, or previous condition of servitude." The Fifteenth Amendment angered radical women's rights leaders, who thought that it would have been quite simple to include the word "sex" along with "race, color, or previous condition of servitude." The exclusion of women from these amendments highlighted the necessity for another amendment extending the vote to women; Stanton predicted that such an amendment would take at least a century to achieve, and she wasn't too far off in her estimation.

Stanton and Anthony did not keep silent about their growing dissatisfaction with what they saw as the capitulation of the AERA to the Republican Party, which was less interested in gaining the vote for women than it was in securing a base of voters in the South, long a Democratic stronghold. The argument that it was the "Negro's hour" did not satisfy Stanton and Anthony, who had already been laboring almost twenty years for women's rights. In 1868, through an alliance with a racist millionaire named George Train, Stanton and Anthony were able to start *The Revolution,* a weekly publication devoted to women's rights; in its pages, Stanton in particular began to issue critiques of the federal amendments that were overly racist. Whereas she had earlier fought for complete equality, she now took an elitist tone, highlighting the superiority of the female vote to that of the uneducated black Southern male. She stated that extending the vote to "ignorant" black and immigrant men was "to exalt ignorance above education, vice above virtue, brutality and barbarism above refinement and religion." Such comments antagonized members of the AERA who believed that women's patience was required as they worked to secure the black man's vote. Stanton and Anthony weren't the only leaders critical of the AERA: Sojourner Truth spoke out against the elevation of black men's rights, saying, "[I]f coloured men get their rights and not coloured women theirs . . . coloured men will be masters over the women . . . I wish woman to have her voice."

By the time the Fifteenth Amendment was ratified in early 1870, the women's movement had already divided. Feeling great distance from members of the AERA who supported the Republicans' plan to secure the vote for black men, in May 1869 Stanton and Anthony formed the National Woman Suffrage Association (NWSA), a group intended for women only, since they thought men in the antislavery movement had consistently betrayed women's interests. In November 1869, Lucy Stone, Henry Blackwell, poet and social activist Julia Ward Howe, and others formed the American Woman Suffrage Association (AWSA). In spite of the division between the groups, one remarkable thing emerged out of the struggle over the enfranchisement of black men: The women's rights movement finally defined itself in terms of suffrage, something it had not done up to that point. Beyond this common self-definition, the two groups were very different. The NWSA, which derived its support from women in upstate New York and the Midwest, focused on the need for a federal amendment, whereas the AWSA, which was based in Boston, worked to get suffrage passed on the state level. The two groups also differed in their philosophies. AWSA was a conservative organization that wished to focus on the one issue of gaining suffrage for women: It was not concerned with the rights of working women, it did not try to challenge the power of churches, and it did not wish to reform marriage laws. In contrast, the NWSA tried to do all of these things; its goals were broader and more radical.

One of the ways the NWSA showed its more radical agenda was through its association with the flamboyant freethinker Victoria Woodhull. The daughter of a drifter father and a spiritualist mother, Woodhull was married at age fifteen to a middle-aged doctor. This marriage led to neither stability nor respectability, however; because her alcoholic husband did not support her or their two children, she continued to travel with her sister, Tennessee Claflin, making money by selling medical cures and spiritual advice. On the road, after meeting and marrying another man—while still married to her first husband, no less—Woodhull moved to New York City, where she and her sister made a fortune on Wall Street by following the stock tips of Commodore Cornelius Vanderbilt. Woodhull came to the attention of the NWSA in early 1871 when she spoke before the House Judiciary Committee, arguing that the Fourteenth and Fifteenth Amendments, because of their use of the words "person" and "citizen," respectively, guaranteed women the right to vote. Impressed with her logic, members of the NWSA invited Woodhull to repeat her speech before their organization, which was holding its annual meeting in the nation's

Liberating the Housewife

Not all women's rights activists at the end of the nineteenth century were fixated on securing the vote for women. Charlotte Perkins Gilman was more concerned with the ways economic dependence steered women into constrained, unfulfilled lives. For Gilman, women's lot could be improved only if societal structures shifted to allow women to develop meaningful work.

Gilman is perhaps best known now for her 1892 short story "The Yellow Wall-Paper," a fictionalized account of her mental breakdown after the birth of her only child. Prescribed the "rest cure" by the physician S. Weir Mitchell, Gilman was forbidden to write, read, or do any intellectual work; while the cure did not take, Gilman's separation and divorce from her husband helped her regain her health and strength. Although she ultimately enjoyed a lasting marriage to her second husband, Gilman defined herself through her work as a writer, critic, speaker, and sociologist rather than through her private role as wife and mother.

While *Herland,* a utopian novel about an all-female society, has become a feminist classic, *Women and Economics* is the book that made Gilman widely known in her time; published in 1898, by 1920 it had gone into nine printings and been translated into seven languages. A believer in evolutionary theory, Gilman argued that, as a result of their dependence on men, women had deteriorated physically, mentally, and morally. Confined to the domestic realm, women performed housework that could be done more efficiently by involving outside professionals, women who were trained to care for children or to cook for large numbers of people in a neighborhood. Gilman proposed that women get jobs and pay others to do their cooking, cleaning, and childcare; indeed, having time away from their children, she believed, would make women better mothers.

Some of Gilman's ideas are eerily prescient of the turn middle-class society has taken these days: Many people with enough money hire someone to clean their houses, cook their meals, and watch their children. Gilman is a significant thinker because of her focus on the economic side of middle-class white women's lives. In addition, she realized the urgency of speaking about the circumstances of married women with children, not just those of single working women or college women. After all, married women were the largest segment of the female population, and proposals for reform needed to take their lives into account.

capital. Although the NWSA invited Woodhull to speak the following year as well, by this point Susan B. Anthony, in particular, had grown wary of Woodhull's self-aggrandizing manner. Whereas Anthony would put into practice the right to vote claimed by Woodhull by casting a ballot in November's presidential election—and would be arrested for this action—Woodhull's goals were more ambitious and self-serving. After deciding to run for president, Woodhull urged the NWSA to support her by creating its own political party with her as its candidate; Anthony rejected this idea, seeing Woodhull as using the NWSA for her own purposes.

Another thing Anthony disliked about Woodhull was her promotion of "free love," or the belief in sex outside of marriage. Woodhull was unabashed in her embrace of the idea, which challenged Victorian codes of sexuality and female passionlessness. In front of a crowd in New York City, she stated, "I have an inalienable, constitutional, and natural right to love whom I may love, to love as long, or as short a period as I can, to change that love every day if I please." While Anthony and some of the more conservative members of the NWSA objected to free love, Elizabeth Cady Stanton supported it, saying, "We have already enough women sacrificed to this sentimental, hypocritical, practicing purity, without going out of our way to increase the number. This is one of man's most effective engines for our division and subjugation." In spite of Stanton's support of a more open attitude toward sexuality, Anthony got the last word, ousting Woodhull from the NWSA so that the organization could concentrate on women's suffrage and not be beholden to the charismatic iconoclast.

Without Woodhull as a distraction, the NWSA and the AWSA both worked separately for suffrage in the 1870s and 1880s. During this time, the social landscape was changing for women. For one thing, around the time of the Civil War, women began to gain access to higher education: The University of Iowa admitted women in 1855 and the University of Wisconsin did the same in 1863. More institutions opened their doors to women after the war: Boston University accepted females at its opening in 1869 and Cornell University did so in 1872. Women's colleges emerged as well, providing female students with a single-sex environment in which to pursue advanced education. Vassar College was founded in 1861, followed by Smith in 1871 and Wellesley in 1875.

Another thing changing by the end of the century was the settlement of the West and the greater freedoms this part of the country afforded to women. Women gained suffrage in the West earlier than they did anywhere else in the country. Although one might think that the "pioneering spirit" of the West led to a questioning of conventional attitudes toward women, in the cases of Wyoming and Utah, legislators extended the vote to women for practical reasons. In an effort to attract female settlers and encourage the development of families and communities, legislators in the Wyoming territory granted women suffrage in 1869, becoming the first place on the continent where women could vote. Because Congress wanted to disenfranchise any man who supported polygamy, leaders of the Mormon church in the Utah territory realized that, with the vote, women could help ward off such meddlesome attacks by outsiders. Interestingly, in approving the law that granted its women the vote in 1870, the territory's governor, a non-Mormon, hoped that female members of the Mormon church would use the franchise for precisely the reverse reason: to stop polygamy. When Wyoming and Utah entered the union, in 1890 and 1896, respectively, they did so as states with female suffrage. By 1896, two other states had granted women the vote: Colorado in 1893 and Idaho in 1896.

By the time there were four woman suffrage states, the split between the two wings of the suffrage movement had been repaired, thanks to the tireless work of Alice Stone Blackwell, the daughter of Lucy Stone. After three years of negotiation between the NWSA and the AWSA, the National American Woman Suffrage Association (NAWSA) was formed in 1890, and Elizabeth Cady Stanton was elected its first president. Although she served the organization for two years, Stanton was growing less interested in suffrage work and more involved in divorce reform and critiques of religion. In 1892, she resigned as president, and Susan B. Anthony took over this position.

"Two More Bright Spots on the Map," by Harry Osborn, charted women's suffrage gains in the Western United States.

The publication of Stanton's *Woman's Bible* in 1895 distanced her from most suffragists, who thought that her reinterpretation of passages from Genesis and Judges was far too extreme. In 1896, in spite of a protest from Anthony, the NAWSA publicly dissociated itself from Stanton's work, thereby severing its ties with the woman who had been among the first to fight for suffrage. Although Anthony would lead the NAWSA from 1892 to 1900, Stanton's departure ushered in a time known as the "Doldrums," a period lasting from 1896 to 1910, when no new suffrage states were gained. Anthony's passionate commitment to suffrage inspired a younger generation of women, some of whom were part of her inner circle. Yet, the thinking of Anthony, who sought a federal amendment, was out of sync with this circle of "nieces," who were more enthusiastic about state-by-state reform.

The suffrage movement at the turn of the twentieth century had very different ideological underpinnings than it had had throughout much of the nineteenth century. Whereas early thinkers such as Wollstonecraft and the Grimkés believed that women deserved the vote because of their natural rights as citizens, women in the early twentieth century didn't make arguments about women's equality. Instead, they claimed that women were different from men and superior to them; as a result, they deserved the vote. This notion of the moral superiority of women conformed with popular late-Victorian views of women and contributed to the mainstreaming of the suffrage movement, which was no longer seen as a radical or fringe movement but as acceptable work for middle-class women to undertake.

Just as Stanton, Anthony, and Stone were the main leaders of the women's rights movement at midcentury, two women—Carrie Chapman Catt and Alice Paul—played pivotal roles in the quest for suffrage in the early twentieth century. These women, however, did not work as partners; indeed, their ideas and tactics were very much at odds. Born in Wisconsin in 1859, Carrie Catt spent most of her formative years in Iowa, attending college at Iowa State University, where she graduated in 1880. After working first as a teacher and then as a principal, Catt became a school superintendent in Mason City, Iowa. Marrying in 1885, Catt quit her job and started editing a column on women's issues for her husband's newspaper. When her husband died suddenly of typhoid fever, Catt moved to California, where she worked in the newspaper business. Her return to Iowa in 1887 marked the beginning of her formal involvement in the women's rights movement; back in her home state, Catt made her living by lecturing on women's rights. She remarried in 1890, but only after securing her husband's promise that she be able to spend one-third of each year on suffrage work.

Catt's involvement in the campaign for suffrage in a number of Western states brought her to the attention of the NAWSA, and she eventually rose through the ranks of the organization to become its president in 1900. Before starting her ascent in the NAWSA, Catt participated in the campaign for a suffrage referendum in South Dakota in 1890; she led the successful campaign in Colorado three years later.

After speaking at the national meeting of the NAWSA in 1890, Catt became the chair of the national Organization Committee in 1895. Although she was not a member of Susan B. Anthony's close circle, the older woman recognized Catt's organizational talents; furthermore, Catt had no children, and Anthony saw this as a benefit since the younger woman could devote all of her energies to the suffrage cause. This was true until 1904, when Catt decided not to seek reelection but instead to take care of herself and her ailing husband, who died the following year. Catt's successor, Anna Howard Shaw, managed the NAWSA until Catt returned to the presidency in 1915.

More radical than Catt was the younger Alice Paul, who learned about activism from the militant suffrage activists she met in England at the turn of the twentieth century. Born into an affluent Quaker family in 1885, Paul advocated nonviolent but militant action in pursuit of her goals. After getting a doctorate in political science at the University of Pennsylvania, Paul moved to England, where she became involved in suffrage activism, participating in public demonstrations and hunger strikes. When she returned to the United States, Paul, along with Lucy Burns, whom she met in jail in England, took over the NAWSA's Congressional Committee (later known as the Congressional Union), whose object it was to focus on the passage of a federal suffrage amendment, also known as the Anthony Amendment. This amendment had been introduced in Congress every year since 1878—to no avail. Paul, Burns, and the young women they recruited worked to lobby congressmen about the necessity for an amendment to the Constitution. Like many of the younger generation of suffragists, Paul was losing patience with the NAWSA's slow tactics. Instead of speaking to women who were already converted to the cause at annual conventions, Paul saw the need for direct action, advocating public demonstrations, parades, and picketing, tactics she learned in England. She also thought that the NAWSA had worked long enough to gain state support of suffrage; she felt the urgent need for the passage—and ratification—of a federal amendment.

One of the first things Paul and Burns did after taking over the

What's in a Name?

Although people today might use the words interchangeably, to people in the early twentieth century the terms "suffragist" and "suffragette" meant different things. Most basically, suffragists were American and suffragettes were British. However, calling a mainstream American activist a suffragette would be more than a mistake; it would be an insult, since the term connoted a kind of militant activism that many American women wanted nothing to do with.

The most famous suffragettes were Englishwoman Emmeline Pankhurst, who founded the Women's Social and Political Union (WSPU) in 1903, and her daughters Christabel and Sylvia. The Pankhursts and their followers were known for their bold actions; they heckled politicians and organized public demonstrations, processions, and mass marches. They even used vandalism to communicate their message; in the name of women's suffrage they smashed store windows, burned public and private property, and slashed oil paintings. One suffragette even killed herself for the cause, throwing herself in front of the king's horse on Derby Day in 1913.

The violence of the WSPU, which advocated "deeds, not words," appalled many people, particularly the established American activists of the NAWSA, who did not believe in such militant tactics. However, because others—most notably Alice Paul, Lucy Burns, and Harriot Stanton Blatch, the daughter of Elizabeth Cady Stanton—were tired of the slow pace of American suffrage activity, they thought they could learn from the techniques of their British sisters and incorporated the suffragettes' militance into their own activism.

Congressional Committee was to organize a suffrage parade to coincide with Woodrow Wilson's inauguration in 1913. Following the lead of British women, American suffragists had been staging parades since 1908, but the Washington parade was different from these spectacles, which had been witnessed by respectful audiences. The parade organized by Paul gained attention because it was exceptionally large: Five thousand women marched in it, and three hundred thousand people reportedly watched it. Instead of passively observing the women's processing through the streets, the crowd got out of control, insulting the women and impeding their progress. Although Paul had secured a police permit for the parade, the police did little to assist the women when they were under attack. The mayhem that ensued because of the police's ineffectiveness brought publicity to the suffrage movement; the public learned about a cause it might have been unaware of and sympathized with the women who were rudely and roughly treated.

Using more dramatic modes of activism was not the only thing Paul and Burns learned in England, however. The Congressional Union adopted the English suffragettes' policy of holding the party in power responsible for women's inferior legal status. In 1914 and 1916, members of the Congressional Union, now referring to themselves as the National Woman's Party, campaigned against Democratic candidates in an effort to unseat the party of President Woodrow Wilson, who had been equivocal in his support of women's suffrage, famously claiming that the issue had never been brought to his attention. In designing this strategy, Paul hoped to speak to the four million women who could already vote and thereby influence the electoral college, one quarter of which was controlled by woman suffrage states. By having women withhold their votes for Democrats, Paul hoped to convey the significance of women's political power. The NAWSA disapproved of Paul's tactics, priding itself on its tradition of nonpartisanship in the fight for the vote. In spite of the intense campaigning of the National Woman's Party, however, Wilson was reelected and Democratic candidates were not defeated; the National Woman's Party's efforts seemed not to have yielded the results for which it had hoped.

Because of her militant tactics, Paul was expelled from the NAWSA in 1915 when Carrie Catt resumed her leadership of the organization. The distance between Paul and the NAWSA only grew when the young leader and her compatriots began to use picketing, a tactic they adopted from the labor movement. Members of the National Woman's Party began to picket the White House, holding banners that asked MR. PRESIDENT, HOW LONG MUST WOMEN WAIT FOR LIBERTY? and MR. PRESIDENT, WHAT WILL YOU DO FOR WOMAN SUFFRAGE? The public protest of Paul's group was nonviolent and silent; instead of speaking, the women let their sharply worded banners communicate for them. Members of the more staid and respectable NAWSA viewed the picketing as undignified and ultimately unhelpful, but the tactic succeeded in capturing the public's attention, particularly when members of Paul's group started to get arrested. When the National Woman's Party continued to picket the White House even after the United States entered into World War I in April 1917, many activists were arrested for obstructing traffic on the sidewalk. Alice Paul, Lucy Burns, and journalist Dorothy Day, among others, were jailed in Occoquan, a workhouse in Virginia, where Paul underwent psychiatric testing and ultimately began a hunger strike, which lasted twenty-two days. When the news broke about the activists' treatment in jail—including the force-feeding of Alice Paul—the public was shocked and outraged, ultimately sympathizing with the women and their cause.

While the NAWSA disapproved of the more radical tactics of the National Woman's Party, the younger and smaller organization—there were fifty thousand members of the National Woman's Party, compared to the two million members of the NAWSA—brought much publicity to the cause of women's suffrage. Even so, the NAWSA played a key role in strategizing for women's suffrage, especially after

Members of the National Woman's Party picketing in front of the White House, February 1917.

Carrie Catt unveiled her "Winning Plan" shortly after her return to the presidency in 1915. Catt's plan included work on a select number of state campaigns but the devotion of most of the NAWSA's energies to gaining a federal amendment. A skillful strategist, Catt wanted to obtain suffrage by 1920, and she thought she could do so by building on the momentum that had begun in 1910, when Washington state passed a suffrage amendment, ending the "Doldrums" period. After this historic amendment, the first in fourteen years, California, Oregon, Arizona, Kansas, Montana, Nevada, and Illinois all passed woman suffrage. Catt wanted to secure a few more states, including one Southern one, and concentrate on achieving a federal amendment. She met with President Wilson repeatedly, working to convince him of the importance of suffrage; by the end of 1915, Wilson had endorsed women's suffrage.

As had been the case in the abolition movement and the suffrage movement after the Civil War, activists in the early-twentieth-century women's suffrage movement divided along racial and ethnic lines. Black women found that they were not welcomed within the mainstream suffrage movement. For instance, in spite of her Quaker background with its commitment to racial equality, Alice Paul did not want to risk alienating Southern supporters when she organized the Washington suffrage parade in 1913. As a result, when the black activist Ida Wells-Barnett, whose outspoken crusade against lynching in the 1890s first brought her to national prominence, wanted to march, Paul explained that she could do so at the back of the parade line with other black women. Wells-Barnett refused to comply with this racist distinction; watching the parade from the street, she joined and marched with the Chicago delegation when it passed by. Like Paul, the NAWSA worried that involving black suffragists in its work would upset Southern activists, who opposed granting suffrage to black women for both racist and political reasons: In some states, such as Louisiana, blacks outnumbered whites. Some suffragists espoused nativist sentiments as well, worried about allegedly "ignorant" immigrants of both sexes. For instance, such people claimed that, because there were more native-born women than immigrant men and women, the votes of native-

The Birth of Birth Control

To think that what we now refer to as "reproductive rights" was of no concern to women before the advent of the Pill, the sexual revolution of the 1960s, and *Roe v. Wade* would be a big mistake. In the nineteenth century, proponents of what was called "voluntary motherhood" argued that women had the right to choose when they wanted to be mothers; practically, this meant that they had the right to refuse their husband's sexual advances—a remarkable feat given the fact that "true women" were expected to submit to their husbands' desires in every way.

At the turn of the twentieth century, women such as the radical anarchist Emma Goldman began to demand sexual freedom for women. Goldman recognized that reliable contraceptives would help increase women's sexual pleasure; instead of worrying about pregnancy, women could actually relax and enjoy sex. To educate women, Goldman distributed information about contraceptive methods and even went to jail for this activity.

Perhaps the most famous advocate for women's sexual autonomy was Margaret Sanger, who learned about contraceptives from Goldman. One of eleven children, Sanger grew up in poverty and understood firsthand how too many children can affect the lives of poor families. After training as a nurse, Sanger worked on the Lower East Side of New York City, where she saw women who were already burdened with too many children getting pregnant and then trying to abort by themselves. The death of one of her patients after a self-induced abortion provided the inspiration Sanger

born women would cancel the votes of the immigrant population. Although people such as activists Harriot Stanton Blatch and Jane Addams opposed such views, Carrie Catt was not above making expedient but bigoted arguments that would win her support among women with biases against immigrants.

Although Jane Addams was less central than Catt or Paul to the struggle to gain suffrage, she was significant for her ability to transcend class and ethnic divisions and ally herself with poor, working, and immigrant women. Born into an affluent family in Illinois in 1860, Addams graduated from Rockford Seminary unprepared for practical needed to change her life's work, becoming a public advocate for "birth control," a term she coined in 1914.

Sanger wrote and distributed *Family Limitation*, a pamphlet written in accessible English and aimed at working-class women. In it, Sanger explained various contraceptive methods, directing her message at women since, in her experience, men were not reliable practitioners of birth control. After learning about the diaphragm during a trip to Holland, Sanger returned to New York, where she opened a clinic. Although the pamphlet was confiscated and her clinic was closed, Sanger continued her work to provide women what they needed—both information and contraceptives themselves—to limit their families. Thanks to Sanger, organizations such as Planned Parenthood, which she founded, exist today.

Although many people recognize the important role Sanger played in educating women about birth control, some have criticized her for her belief in eugenics. A social view popular in the early twentieth century, eugenics is the study of the hereditary improvement of humans by controlled selective breeding. Proponents of eugenics argued that, through euthanasia, sterilization, and birth control, those who were seen as genetically "unfit" would not be permitted to reproduce. While Sanger did not believe that the state had a right to create a "master race," she did want women to learn about contraception so they could make reproductive choices for themselves. As she put it, an individual woman has the right to decide "whether she shall bear children or not, and how many children she shall bear if she chooses to become a mother."

work, uninterested in marriage, and unable to find a meaningful application for her education. After a long period of searching, Addams finally found a way to combat her "sense of futility and misdirected energy." Inspired by a visit to London's Toynbee Hall, a settlement house that improved the lives of the poor, Addams returned to the United States, where she and her friend Ellen Starr bought Hull House, an abandoned mansion in the Chicago slums. There, Addams started the first American settlement house and helped initiate and professionalize the field of social work. Initially, Addams was as determined to use Hull House as a source of satisfaction for other women in her situation as she was to benefit the poor and working-class members of the community. Although she first saw the settlement house as a site for charity and philanthropy, Hull House grew to offer practical services, such as kindergartens and English classes, that improved the lives of immigrant communities in concrete ways.

As Addams attracted more and more people to Hull House, such as the labor reformer Florence Kelley, she started to see her work in terms of eradicating poverty instead of providing palliative care to the poor. Addams's association with the labor organizers Mary Kenny O'Sullivan and Mary Anderson, for example, introduced her to working women who needed trade unions to make their lives more bearable. Addams attended trade union meetings, and she was among the group of women who organized the Women's Trade Union League in 1903. Of a practical rather than theoretical turn of mind, Addams fought for improved housing, schools, and labor conditions for the nation's urban poor. Since she believed that these goals could be achieved legislatively, it is not surprising that Addams supported women's suffrage; working women deserved to be able to make their voices heard and, in so doing, create laws that would benefit and protect them. Addams spoke out actively on behalf of women and the vote; she served as first vice president of the NAWSA between 1911 and 1914.

Because of the work of committed people such as Addams, Catt, and Paul, the suffrage amendment made its way to Congress once again, this time poised for victory. In January 1918, Jeannette Rankin, a representative from Montana and the first female member of Congress, reintroduced the Anthony Amendment to the House floor. The amendment passed, with 274 people in favor of it and 136 against it. After much difficulty in the Senate, the amendment passed there one and a half years later. Once this happened, members of the NAWSA worked at the state level to ensure that the ratification process would succeed. On August 26, 1920, Tennessee became the thirty-sixth and final state to ratify the Nineteenth Amendment. The final and deciding vote in Tennessee belonged to twenty-four-year-old Harry Burns, who changed his vote after receiving a telegram from his mother reminding him to "be a good boy" and "vote for suffrage." After a long, hard battle, women finally had won the vote; because the struggle took so many years, most of the original activists, including Elizabeth Cady Stanton and Susan B. Anthony, were not alive to see this victory. Indeed, only one of the original signers of the Declaration of Sentiments from 1848, Charlotte Woodward, survived to see this day. Although her failing health made her unable to vote in 1920, the next year, when she was 92 years old, she donated a trowel to be used in building the National Woman's Party's headquarters in Washington, DC. The trowel's inscription read: "In memory of the Seneca Falls Convention in 1848: presented by its sole survivor . . . in thanksgiving for progress made by women and in honor of the National Woman's Party, which will carry on the struggle so bravely begun."

"The Sky Is Now Her Limit," by Bushnell, appeared a few months after the Nineteenth Amendment was ratified in 1920.

Chapter 3

Second Wave Feminism: Seeking Liberation and Equality

On August 26, 1970, to commemorate the fiftieth anniversary of the ratification of the Nineteenth Amendment, women's rights activists organized the Women's Strike for Equality. The brainchild of Betty Friedan, the first president of the National Organization for Women (NOW) and the author of the best-selling *The Feminine Mystique,* the nationwide strike dramatized women's unwillingness to maintain traditional gender roles in a changing world. In conceiving of the twenty-four-hour general strike, Friedan wanted to display the "resistance both passive and active, of all women in America against the concrete conditions of their oppression." Although women had gained the vote in 1920, they still experienced oppression in various ways, many of which stemmed from the fact that society thought of them primarily as wives and mothers, roles that had little status in mainstream society and even less monetary remuneration. The "concrete conditions" of their lives in 1970 can be easily listed: If they worked outside the home, as 44 percent of women did, they could not rely on childcare centers, since very few of these existed. They could expect to make much less than their husbands; on average, women earned 52 cents to the dollar men made. Married women could not get a credit card without their husband's permission; they didn't even have their own credit rating. If a woman needed help after her husband hit her, she could find little assistance both because domestic violence was not discussed in public—the term had not been coined yet—and because almost no shelters existed to house battered women. Single women had a hard time renting an apartment on their own, just as they might find it difficult to get served in a restaurant or bar. Whether they were single or married, women had less opportunity than they wanted.

The organizers of the strike—both liberal feminists, who wanted to reform existing institutions to make them more equitable to women, and radical feminists, who sought to challenge sexist institutions such as marriage and the family—put aside their ideological differences and agreed on three key demands: the right to safe and legal abortion, the right to accessible and affordable childcare, and equal opportunities in education and employment. In towns and cities across the country, women held rallies and teach-ins; they also picketed, marched, and protested, many in creative ways. For instance, in Boston, women chained themselves to an enormous typewriter; in Berkeley, they marched carrying pots and pans on their backs; in Rochester, New York, they shattered teacups to signal their displeasure at women's lack of participation in government.

The largest demonstration occurred in New York City, where, depending on whose records you consult, between twenty thousand and fifty thousand women marched down Fifth Avenue holding banners and posters, some of which read DON'T COOK DINNER—STARVE A RAT TODAY and DON'T IRON WHILE THE STRIKE IS HOT. All kinds of women—young mothers, suburban housewives, college students, office workers, and even elderly suffrage activists—participated in the protest. The biggest women's action since the parades of the suffrage movement, the Women's Strike for Equality succeeded in capturing the attention of the media and, thus, the country; in so doing, it communicated the desires of a new women's movement to a nation familiar with social unrest but largely unready for the seismic shift in gender relations already being legislated in the halls of government and beginning to play out in kitchens and bedrooms across America. The Women's Strike did not inaugurate the second wave of the women's movement; liberal feminism originated in the early 1960s. However, the spectacle of the Women's Strike, particularly in New York, visually echoed the suffrage parades earlier in the century, which announced women's demands in a clear, public way. What had been happening in women's lives that they felt the need—fifty years after gaining the vote—to demand their rights in a similarly public way?

One way to answer this question is to think about what happened to the women's movement after the ratification of the Nineteenth Amendment in 1920. Did a new generation of talented activists emerge to take the places of Carrie Chapman Catt and Alice Paul? In what ways did this younger generation seek to improve the lives of women in the twentieth century? In part, the social freedoms women gained during the 1920s may have distracted some women from activism. The individualism of the "Roaring Twenties," with its culture of self-indulgence and its focus on personal and corporate wealth, may have contributed to the disappearance of the women's movement.

Yet it would be wrong to place exclusive blame on the social climate of the time. Another reason for the decline of the women's movement was the fact that, after 1890, activists had devoted nearly all of their attention to gaining the vote. As a result, once suffrage was achieved, the movement had no other unifying goals; its raison d'être had vanished. Indeed, after the ratification of the Nineteenth Amendment, the National American Woman Suffrage Association (NAWSA) ceased to exist as the institutional home for women's rights activism; in its place Carrie Catt founded the League of Women Voters, whose goals were educational and nonpartisan. Many suffragists who might have embarked upon careers in elected office instead became involved in the league's work of educating women for citizenship. In addition to teaching women about the political process, the league also worked at the state level for the passage of legislation it saw as crucial to women's lives, supporting laws pertaining to child welfare, education, women's labor and living conditions, and racial injustice.

After forming a coalition called the Women's Joint Congressional Committee with mainstream and professional groups such as the General Federation of Women's Clubs, the National Consumers

League, the National Federation of Business and Professional Women's Clubs, and the American Association of University Women, the League of Women Voters began to exert its power as a lobbying group in Washington. Perhaps its biggest success, qualified as it turned out to be, was the passage of the Sheppard-Towner Maternity and Infancy Protection Act in 1921. Introduced by Representative Jeannette Rankin in 1918, the act provided matching funds to states to assist poor women with the pre- and postnatal care of infants. Although the bill was extended in 1927, the legislation lapsed in 1929, both because of the onset of the Depression and because women were not voting in numbers high enough to be considered a "bloc" that really mattered to politicians. In spite of the league's early concern with issues affecting women, as time went on, the organization grew less and less interested in identifying itself with feminism; in fact, by the late 1940s, members of the league preferred to think of themselves as "citizens first and as women incidentally."

Unlike most members of the League of Women Voters, Alice Paul, the head of the National Woman's Party, never stopped defining her work in an explicitly feminist way. Shortly after the ratification of the Nineteenth Amendment, she identified a new issue that would dominate the rest of her life. In 1923, in honor of the seventy-fifth anniversary of the Seneca Falls Convention, she introduced the Lucretia Mott Amendment, which read: "Men and women shall have equal rights throughout the United States and every place subject to its jurisdiction." Known subsequently as the Alice Paul Amendment and later as the Equal Rights Amendment (ERA), it was introduced in Congress every year. Although succinctly, even innocently, phrased, Paul's amendment led to a sharp division in the women's movement that contributed to its loss of power. On one side of the division were the more radical or political feminists who supported the ERA. In favor of clearing the way constitutionally for women's equal access to all opportunities in the public sphere, these women believed that the ERA would elevate women's status both legally and symbolically. On the other side of the debate were reformist or social feminists, who thought of women not just in terms of their access to professions; instead, organizations such as the League of Women Voters, the National Consumers League, and the Women's Trade Union League tended to see women in terms of their roles as mothers. For these groups, the Equal Rights Amendment threatened to eliminate legislation that could protect women; instead of favoring an abstract equality of the sexes, social feminists wanted to ensure the viability of laws safeguarding mothers' and infants' health, laws restricting child labor, and laws regulating women's working hours and conditions. Indeed, many people saw the Equal Rights Amendment as elitist; concerned mainly with professional women's access to the public realm, it showed little interest in the working-class women who needed protection from unfair labor practices. The single-minded agenda of the National Woman's Party in working for the passage of the ERA alienated many women; while the party had thirty-five thousand members in 1920, by 1930 only one thousand women maintained membership in the organization.

By 1930, the Great Depression had set in, and, out of necessity, most American women turned away from women's rights activism and devoted their energies to physical survival. Some women, such as Esther Peterson and Maida Springer, whom historian Dorothy Sue Cobble refers to as social justice feminists, advocated for the survival of working women. Others, such as Dorothy Day and Meridel LeSueur, combined activism with writing about the cause of poor women. Many of these women became involved in the Communist movement. These women were the exceptions, however; it was only when the economic and political fortunes of the country stabilized after World War II that more women resumed work on behalf of their sex. Still, most refused to identify themselves as "feminists." In 1947, the year after the League of Women Voters rejected any connection with a feminist movement, the Women's Bureau in the Department of Labor, since 1920 a bastion of social feminism, tried to distance its agenda from feminism and "equal rights." The National Woman's Party was the only group to refer to itself as "feminist" during the period from 1920 to 1960. As the Cold War intensified, female activists may have rejected

Women Know a Lot of Things

Born in 1900, Meridel Le Sueur participated in the working-class and Communist movements of the 1930s and '40s. Appearing in proletarian publications such as *New Masses*, her writing was not widely known outside these movements until second wave feminists discovered her work in the 1970s. The following excerpt is from an essay called "Women Know a Lot of Things," which appears in *Ripening*, a collection of Le Sueur's work published in 1982.

Women know a lot of things they don't read in the newspapers. It's pretty funny sometimes, how women know a lot of things and nobody can figure out how they know them. I know a Polish woman who works in the stockyards here, and she has been working there for a good many years. She came from Poland when she was a child, came across the vast spaces of America, with blinders on, you might say, and yet she knows more than anybody I know, because she knows what suffering is and she knows that everyone is like herself, throughout the whole world. . . .

That's the way it is with women. They don't read about the news. They very often make it. They pick it up at its source, in the human body, in the making of the body, and the feeding and nurturing of it day in and day out. They know how much a body weighs and how much blood and toil goes into the making of even a poor body. Did you ever go into a public clinic to weigh your child? And you feel of him anxiously when you put his clothes on in the morning. You pick him up trying to gauge

the term as a way to protect themselves from the anti-Communist paranoia endemic to the nation. To people who knew little about either feminism or Communism, both philosophies challenged traditional social norms and threatened the American way of life. During the heyday of Senator Joseph McCarthy's hunt for Communists, people wanted to look "normal" and not raise any suspicions; being perceived *the weight of his bones and the tiny flesh and you wait for the public nurses to put him on the scales, and you look, you watch her face like an aviator watches the sky, watches an instrument register a number that will mean life and death.*

In that body under your hands every day there resides the economy of the world; it tells you of ruthless exploitation, of a mad, vicious class that now cares for nothing in the world but to maintain its stupid life with violence and destruction; it tells you the prices of oranges and cod liver oil, of spring lamb, of butter, eggs and milk. You know everything that is happening on the stock exchange. You know what happened to last year's wheat in the drouth, the terrible misuse and destruction of land and crops and human life plowed under. You don't have to read the stock reports in Mr. Hearst's paper. You have the news at its terrible source.

Or what kind of news is it when you see the long, drawn face of your husband coming home from the belt line and feel his ribs coming to the surface day after day like the hulk of a ship when the tide is going down?

Or, what price freedom and the American Way so coyly pictured on the billboards, when you go up the dark and secret and dirty stairs to a doctor's office and get a cheap abortion because you can't afford another baby and wait for the fever that takes so many American women, and thank heaven if you come through alive, barely crawling around for months?

. . . Hunger and want and terror are a Braille that hands used to labor, used to tools, and close to sources, can read in any language.

as different could lead to being labeled a Communist. Yet, in spite of the skittishness surrounding the term "feminism," women in the 1940s and '50s were involved with activist projects, including peace, labor, and social reform movements.

When the United States entered World War II, women's lives changed dramatically. Not only did women forge new family structures as fathers, husbands, and brothers fought abroad but they participated in the war themselves as uniformed personnel and nurses. More commonly, to fill the jobs vacated by the twelve million men who joined the armed forces, women left the domestic realm, some taking positions they never thought they could. While many women performed clerical, service, and retail work, others, influenced by the image of Rosie the Riveter, the star of a government propaganda campaign aimed to convince women of the patriotic nature of industrial work, found more lucrative employment in heavy industry. After being trained to drill, hammer, and rivet, these workers gained experience manufacturing machinery, armaments, aircrafts, and ships. Many women experienced great satisfaction not just as a result of the good wages they earned in their industrial jobs but because of the skills and competence they acquired through this unconventional work. While propaganda posters depicting Rosie as a well-groomed, even glamorous, white woman created the idea that the women who took on these "masculine" jobs were lured away from sheltered domesticity, the often-overlooked reality is that many Rosies were already employed before the war, often as poorly paid domestics in the case of the many African American women who became industrial workers.

The National Archives

J. Howard Miller's "We Can Do It!" poster showed the economic strength many women found in World War II–era manufacturing jobs.

Although 36 percent of women aged sixteen to sixty-five worked outside the home at the height of World War II, once the war ended, many women left the workforce and returned to lives of domesticity or to the more mundane, lower-paying work they had performed before the war began. Some women made this transition willingly; others, most notably women engaged in heavy industry, were fired from their manufacturing jobs to make room for veterans who needed work. In the immediate postwar period, in a desire to reestablish the "normalcy" of domesticity, most middle-class men and women reverted to a conventional division of labor, with men as breadwinners and women as homemakers. It would be incorrect, however, to assume that all men and women freely chose these roles; social, economic, political, and cultural forces made people believe that such roles were normal, desirable, and necessary.

Domesticity was celebrated in the postwar years as it had been in the Victorian era. Even if they had enjoyed their wartime labor, women were asked to make their families and homes the center of their lives. Women's magazines reinforced domesticity by including information that would enable their readers to maintain a comfortable home; these periodicals instructed women on everything from doing laundry and preparing meals to arranging flowers and supervising children. Ads in these magazines presented products whose use would simplify the domestic woman's life; images of washing machines, dishwashers, and refrigerators enticed women to buy goods whose very existence affirmed their participation in an ideal way of life. In the postwar world, the cultural landscape changed as Americans embraced the security that family life seemed to offer. Women married at younger and younger ages and had larger and larger families; having three or four children was extremely common, as it had not been during the Depression, when economic constraints limited family size. Young families populated the suburbs that sprang up, living the "American Dream" of economic security signaled by home ownership and the possession of durable goods such as automobiles and home appliances.

Not everyone had access to this postwar American Dream, however. Black people in the South faced particularly harsh racial discrimination: Not only could they not vote, but their children could not attend schools with white children, they could not sit where they wanted on public buses, and they could not expect service at many hotels, bars, and restaurants. On December 1, 1955, when Rosa Parks, a seamstress in

Montgomery, Alabama, sat in a seat for "whites only," she set in motion a mass movement to protest racial segregation. The bus boycott launched by Parks's action lasted for 381 days and ended only when the local ordinance segregating the races was removed. In Little Rock, Arkansas, nine students desegregated Central High School in 1957. Under the protection of federal troops, the "Little Rock Nine" entered the school building, where white students spat on and even attacked them. Starting in 1960, young people participated in sit-ins; in Greensboro, North Carolina; Nashville; and Atlanta, black students "sat in" at the "white only" lunch counters of local drugstores. The students' nonviolent protests often prompted violent responses from white authorities. After being arrested, protesters refused to post bail, garnering more attention for their cause. In 1960, participants in the sit-ins formed the Student Nonviolent Coordinating Committee (SNCC) to continue their activism; many members of SNCC joined with activists in the Congress of Racial Equality (CORE), who organized freedom rides in 1961. Aimed at testing a recent Supreme Court decision prohibiting segregation at interstate bus terminals, the freedom rides included black and white activists who rode around the South. When a bus was burned in Anniston, Alabama, and riders were attacked in Birmingham and Montgomery, the public in other parts of the country grew outraged at the way the activists were treated. The civil rights movement that began in the 1950s and blossomed in the 1960s set the stage for women's rights reform. As many historians have pointed out, feminist activism has thrived when the cultural climate is generally conducive to reform; just as the first wave of the women's movement arose alongside—indeed, out of—abolition, civil rights work in the 1960s led to a culture more ready to fight for women's rights.

Change certainly was needed, since all was not well inside the ranch houses of suburbia. In March 1960, a cover story in *Newsweek* titled "Young Wives with Brains: Babies, Yes—But What Else?" reported the boredom and discontent of American housewives. Just a few months later, when *Redbook* advertised a $500 prize for the best essay on the topic "Why Young Mothers Feel Trapped," the magazine received twenty-four thousand responses. A Gallup poll from 1962 found that 90 percent of housewives wanted their daughters to have better educations and marry later than they themselves did. However, nothing documented the malaise of the white middle-class suburban housewife more powerfully than Betty Friedan's *The Feminine Mystique*. Raised in a middle-class family in Illinois, Friedan attended Smith College and later worked as a journalist for a left-wing news service and a union publication. After marrying in 1947, Friedan spent most of the 1950s raising three children and doing freelance writing. In researching a magazine story about her graduating class at Smith, Friedan discovered that many of her peers in the class of 1942 felt dissatisfied with the direction their lives had taken. Intrigued by this discovery, Friedan continued her research, and the book she published in 1963 exposed the unhappiness experienced by affluent American women said to have it all—adoring husbands, smiling children, and beautiful homes replete with every modern convenience. Ensconced in homes in the suburbs, these educated white women were bored, unhappy, even hopeless about the future. Friedan described the emptiness of their lives: "As she made the beds, shopped for groceries, matched slipcover material, ate peanut butter sandwiches with her children, chauffeured Boy Scouts and Brownies, [and] lay beside her husband at night—she was afraid to ask even of herself the silent question—'Is this all?'" Friedan labeled the housewife's discontent "the problem that has no name"; according to Friedan, this "problem" was not a result of personal inadequacy or psychological weakness but was caused by the cultural ideology of the feminine mystique, the belief that women should derive fulfillment exclusively through domesticity. In her exposé of the feminine mystique, Friedan blamed educational institutions, women's magazines, advertising, and Freudian psychology for their role in confining women to lives of unfulfilled domesticity.

Although *The Feminine Mystique* caused many women to reevaluate the social roles they had accepted, often uncritically, it did not offer a public policy solution to "the problem that has no name." Even before the publication of Friedan's book, however, a group within the U.S. government had taken up the "woman question": In late 1961, prompted by Esther Peterson, the head of the Women's Bureau in the Department of Labor, and former First Lady Eleanor Roosevelt, President John F. Kennedy formed a Commission on the Status of Women, charging its members—fifteen women and eleven men—to create "recommendations for overcoming discriminations in government and private employment on the basis of sex." For President Kennedy, whose sentiments were not especially feminist and who had not, in fact, named any women to his cabinet, the commission was likely a response to Cold War competition with the Russians and the perceived need to put women's talents to public use. To that end, he asked the commission to "make studies of all barriers to the full participation of women in our democracy." After collecting data, the commission released its *Presidential Report on American Women* in 1963. While the report supported women's traditional roles as wives, mothers, and homemakers, it also acknowledged the fact that, in spite of the feminine mystique, women were increasingly joining the workforce and encountering discrimination there. In addition to demanding better childcare for families, the report documented pay inequality: Women earned as much as 40 percent less than men did for doing the same job. Although the report did not lead to immediate change in women's lives—not least because it appeared in print just a month before President Kennedy's assassination—the presidential commission opened a dialogue about women's place in American society and spawned state commissions that studied women's status in greater depth at the local level.

Even before the commission published its report in October 1963, Congress passed and President Kennedy signed the Equal Pay Act. Although the legislation's original language demanded equal pay for comparable work, the bill President Kennedy signed was considerably diluted, requiring equal pay only for the same work. This new phrasing troubled women's rights activists, who knew that, because jobs were segregated by sex, the law would mean very little since female workers did "women's work" and not the "same work" specified by the law. That is, feminists understood that jobs disproportionately done by women—as nurses or secretaries, for example—pay less than jobs involving the same level of skills and responsibilities but usually performed by men. Yet, in spite of this significant change in wording and the fact that the law did not apply to companies with fewer than twenty-five workers or to agricultural, domestic, executive, administrative, or professional workers, the Equal Pay Act represented a step in the right direction, getting on the books a crucial principle that would pave the way for future legislation and executive orders.

Other legislation from the mid-1960s helped women in the workplace. The passage of Title VII of the Civil Rights Act of 1964 and the establishment of the Equal Employment Opportunity Commission (EEOC) meant that there would be consequences for discriminating against women on the job. The history of this legislation indicates that it came about almost by accident. When Howard Smith, an elderly congressman from Virginia, introduced a change to the civil rights bill under debate in the House of Representatives in early 1964, he did so to derail the bill's passage. Smith suggested including the word "sex" in Title VII, which forbade workplace discrimination on the basis of "race, color, religion, or national origin." Smith, a Democrat and a segregationist, hoped that what he saw as a laughable inclusion to a set of employment regulations would give conservative Northern legislators a way to vote down the bill without looking racist. Smith did not count on the readiness of Congresswoman Martha Griffiths, a Democrat from Michigan, to organize a coalition that would fight for the passage of Title VII and the bill as a whole. The amendment to Title VII passed the House with a vote of 168 to 133, and the entire bill passed 290 to 130. After its passage in the Senate, President Lyndon B. Johnson signed the bill into law on July 2, 1964.

To enforce Title VII, Congress created a new agency, the EEOC, that would investigate complaints about racial and sexual discrimination in the workplace. However, even though the commission received thousands of complaints about sex discrimination in its first year, the EEOC did not take these cases seriously, concentrating instead on race-

Naming a Nine-to-Five Problem

Sometimes it's hard to believe that words and concepts we take for granted as part of everyday vocabulary actually have a history, a point of origin. For instance, in the 1970s, second wave feminists popularized terms such as "Ms." and "domestic violence." They also coined "sexual harassment," though the practice had been around for a very long time, indeed.

In 1975, Carmita Wood, a former office worker at Cornell University in Ithaca, New York, went to the institution's Human Affairs program for assistance. Wood had experienced repeated, unwelcome advances from a male professor. When the faculty member stood near her, he jiggled his crotch or brushed against her breasts; he even kissed her in the elevator one night after an office Christmas party. Wood developed chronic pain, likely as a result of the stress of keeping away from this man. When her requests to be transferred to another job in the university were denied, she quit. She wanted the staff at Human Affairs to help her appeal the rejection of her unemployment benefits.

Wood's situation resonated with staff members Lin Farley, Karen Sauvigne, and Susan Meyer. In addition to finding lawyers to handle Wood's case, the women decided to hold a speak-out to expose this issue to the public. The only problem was that, in making posters for the event, they weren't sure what to call these unwelcome sexual advances. Although they tried out phrases such as "sexual intimidation" and "sexual coercion," it was only when someone suggested "sexual harassment" that they realized they had found the right term.

based grievances. Women activists realized the extent of the EEOC's apathy—and even hostility—to the idea of sex discrimination when it upheld the legality of sex-segregated want ads in 1966. This ruling meant that newspaper job ads would continue to separate postings into men's listings for lawyers, engineers, managers, and accountants and women's listings for domestics, secretaries, nurses, and teachers. This practice reinforced job segregation by sex and taught women to look for work within proper, "feminine" occupations.

When this ruling occurred, many women were frustrated with

On May 4, 1975, almost three hundred women attended the speak-out in Ithaca. Speakers—who ran the gamut of jobs from waitress and factory shop steward to secretary and professor—informed the audience of the harassment they had experienced, everything from physical touching to propositions for sex to verbal threats. The speak-out caught the attention of the *New York Times*, which several months later ran a story called "Women Begin to Speak Out Against Sexual Harassment at Work." This publicity gave the issue of sexual harassment a legitimacy and credibility it desperately needed. Women's magazines started to run stories and survey their readers about the phenomenon. The legal scholar Catharine MacKinnon wrote an important book on the subject, *Sexual Harassment of Working Women*. Even Hollywood got in on the act; the comedy *9 to 5*, starring Jane Fonda, Lily Tomlin, and Dolly Parton, dramatized the sexual harassment experienced by Parton's character, a secretary.

Because victims of sexual harassment face so much risk in filing a complaint against a coworker or boss, it was important to create rules to free the workplace of sexual harassment. As director of the EEOC, Eleanor Holmes Norton did just that, issuing "Guidelines on Discrimination Because of Sex" in 1980. These guidelines stated that sexual activity that was made a condition of employment or promotion could be prosecuted under Title VII; also illegal was the creation of a hostile work environment. As the EEOC guidelines pointed out, "[P]revention is the best tool for the elimination of sexual harassment"; realizing the importance of the guidelines and hoping to avoid any costly litigation, corporations began to develop sensitivity-training programs and harassment guidelines of their own.

the EEOC's implementation of Title VII; one of the most vocal, Representative Martha Griffiths, condemned the EEOC for "its arbitrary arrogance, disregard of the law and hostility to the human rights of women." Also angry were members of the state commissions on the status of women, who happened to be having their annual conference in Washington DC in June 1966. Some commissioners met in Betty Friedan's hotel room one night to discuss a resolution demanding the enforcement of Title VII, but when conference officials did not support the statement the next day, it became apparent that there was a need for a nongovernmental watchdog group to advocate for women's civil rights. At lunch on the final day of the conference, Friedan and the other supporters of the resolution decided to form such a group. Calling it the National Organization for Women (NOW), the women stated that its goal would be "to take action to bring women into full participation in the mainstream of American society now, assuming all the privileges and responsibilities thereof in truly equal partnership with men." Four months later, these women returned to Washington to hold the first meeting of NOW; Betty Friedan was named the organization's president. Although NOW had only three hundred members at this point, its founding was significant both because it was the first women's rights organization created after suffrage and because, in taking control of feminist reform from the federal government, it made activism on behalf of women its top—indeed, its exclusive—priority.

Thirty charter members attended the National Organization for Women's organizing conference, October 29–30, 1966.

As the home of liberal feminism, NOW aimed to work within the system to gain women's legal equality. While NOW has the reputation of devoting its energies to elevating the status of white, middle-class women by securing their access to politics, business, and the professions, the organization included black women and their interests right from the beginning. Indeed, among the founders of NOW were the outspoken and charismatic attorney Flo Kennedy and Pauli Murray, the lawyer who cowrote "Jane Crow and the Law," an early essay on legal discrimination. After Betty Friedan left the presidency of NOW, she was succeeded by Aileen Hernandez, a member of the EEOC. Another early member of NOW, Shirley Chisholm, had an active political career. Born to working-class parents in New York, Chisholm graduated from Brooklyn College in 1946 and worked in a childcare center while earning her master's degree at Columbia University. In 1964, Chisholm ran for the state assembly; after four years, she became the first black woman elected to the U.S. House of Representatives. In 1972, Chisholm made another historic move, becoming the first black woman to seek the Democratic Party's nomination for president. Although she lost this bid, she wrote later that she attempted to run "to demonstrate the sheer will and refusal to accept the status quo." While she was not affiliated with NOW, Eleanor Holmes Norton worked to reform the system, thereby showing her connection with the liberal feminism endorsed by NOW. The daughter of a civil servant father and schoolteacher mother, Norton graduated from Antioch College in 1960 and then entered Yale University, where she earned a law degree. Involved with SNCC in 1963, Norton claims she was "radicalized by the Civil Rights Movement." After clerking for a federal judge, Norton took a position as assistant legal director for the American Civil Liberties Union, where she represented sixty female employees of *Newsweek* who accused the magazine of discrimination against women. A founding member of the National Black Feminist Organization, Norton became the chair of the EEOC during the Carter administration. Because they had worked alongside white women to end poverty and racism, these professional women shared a history of collective struggle with the women who formed the first liberal feminist organizations.

In some of its activism, NOW advocated the rights of ordinary working women. For instance, it supported a lawsuit filed by female flight attendants, who had to retire when they married or turned thirty-two, whichever came first; male flight attendants were subject to no such policy. While the youthfulness of female flight attendants helped make the job—and flying itself—seem glamorous in the 1950s and '60s, age limits were discriminatory, providing airlines a way to maximize their profits by continually hiring young, inexperienced, and lower-paid women to replace retiring workers. NOW also supported a class action lawsuit against Southern Bell, which hired women only as telephone operators instead of as linesmen, who formed the personnel pool for management positions. When Loreen Weeks applied to be a linesman, she was denied the position; the U.S. Fifth Circuit Court ruled that, in order to legally deny Weeks employment, Southern Bell had to show that there was a bona fide occupational qualification Weeks did not possess. In settling the suit, Southern Bell paid $15 million in back pay and $23 million in raises to the women in the lawsuit. NOW also protested the practice of sex-segregated want ads by picketing the *New York Times* office in August 1967 and then by having individual NOW chapters picket local EEOC offices. In August 1968, the EEOC finally outlawed sex-segregated employment ads. NOW also succeeded in pressuring the president to amend Executive Order 11246, which prohibited race-based discrimination in federal employment and in companies with federal contracts. To make this order align with Title VII, President Johnson signed Executive Order 11375 in 1967; this order outlawed sex discrimination in federal employment and in companies with federal contracts. It also required these companies to take affirmative action to make sure that their hiring represented women's availability in the labor pool under consideration.

In spite of the almost immediate gains made by NOW, the organization experienced internal conflict on a number of issues. At its second conference in November 1967, members adopted a Bill of Rights for 1968 but not without sharp disagreement over two of its planks: the ERA and reproductive freedom. Although individual women from the labor movement supported the ERA, their unions, worried that the ERA would eradicate legislation that protected women workers, opposed it; NOW's endorsement of the amendment meant that these women would have to resign from NOW or take a less active role in the organization. NOW's support for the repeal of abortion laws struck some women as too extreme; these women, some of whom went on to found the more moderate

Women's Equity Action League (WEAL), preferred the idea of regulating abortion by reforming abortion statutes rather than repealing them, which would make abortion, at least in theory, available to everyone.

The next year, at NOW's third annual conference, tensions between liberal and radical feminists in the organization boiled over when nine members of the New York NOW chapter publicly severed their ties with the organization. These women, calling themselves the October 17th Movement, were led by Ti-Grace Atkinson, a member of a wealthy Republican family from Louisiana. Educated at the University of Pennsylvania, Atkinson had a strong sense of her intellectual abilities and wanted to prove her radicalism. As president of the New York chapter, Atkinson proposed an egalitarian power-sharing plan whereby "decision making would be chosen by lot and rotated frequently." When Atkinson's decentralized plan was rejected in favor of maintaining the organization's hierarchical model, Atkinson and her supporters walked out. According to radical feminists such as Atkinson, NOW's organizational structure merely replicated the hierarchies of patriarchy; instead, radical feminists wanted to break down these hierarchies and see the world anew. Although the October 17th Movement (later called The Feminists) wasn't the first radical feminist group, its separation from NOW highlighted the difficulties liberal and radical feminists had understanding each other's priorities, goals, and points of view.

The earliest examples of radical feminism, or women's liberation, as it was known, emerged as a response to the sexism of the New Left, the antiwar, and the civil rights movements of the 1960s. The New Left refers to the left-wing social and political activism of the 1960s. Unlike the "Old Left" of the 1930s and '40s, which focused primarily on labor activism, the New Left was a countercultural movement peopled mostly by college students who developed critiques of authority and the alienation that resulted from contemporary capitalist culture. The main organization of the New Left was Students for a Democratic Society (SDS); in the group's core document, "The Port Huron Statement," its author, Tom Hayden, called for "participatory democracy" that would enable "the individual [to] share in those social decisions determining the quality and direction of his life." Rather than becoming involved in electoral politics, members of SDS wanted to transform society by critiquing the way "late capitalist society creates mechanisms of psychological and cultural domination over everyone." Members of SDS spearheaded nonviolent protests in multiple arenas— in favor of free speech and civil rights and against war. SDS ultimately became identified with activism against the Vietnam War; it hoped to "build a democratic and humane society in which Vietnams are unthinkable, in which human life and initiative are precious." Like men, women were attracted to the idealism of groups such as SDS. Inspired by the intellectual fervor and humanistic passion of the New Left, many women grew disillusioned when they started to see that their status within an allegedly radical organization mirrored their status in society as a whole. As the New Left activist Robin Morgan described it in her introduction to *Sisterhood Is Powerful,* "Thinking we were involved in the struggle to build a new society, it was a slowly dawning and depressing realization that we were doing the same work *in* the Movement as out of it: typing the speeches men delivered, making coffee but not policy, being accessories to . . . men."

Similarly, involvement in civil rights activism was initially exhilarating for the many white Northern and Southern women who worked with the Student Nonviolent Coordinating Committee (SNCC). Through their work with SNCC, which organized sit-ins, freedom rides, and voter registration campaigns, women gained experience organizing, doing administrative tasks, and running offices. Although they were committed to ending racism, believing in the "beloved community" of collective, interracial struggle, gradually some white women felt frustrated with their exclusion from leadership in SNCC. Instead of writing position papers and participating in community organizing, activities performed by black, and sometimes white, men, white women typed correspondence, answered phones, mimeographed papers, and arranged meetings. In contrast, black women headed their own projects and did less administrative work than white women. The discrepancy in power in SNCC became especially acute during Freedom Summer in 1964, when three hundred white women arrived in Mississippi to participate in voter registration drives; the ensuing sexual pairings of white women and black men made some women—both white and black—uncomfortable and highlighted women's inequality in the organization.

During Freedom Summer, some black male activists perceived white female volunteers as sexually loose or "easy," and they even used sex with white women to assert their masculinity. Staughton Lynd, a white civil rights activist, sympathized with the white female volunteers, saying that most black men in SNCC "counted it as a notch on [their] gun to have slept with a white woman—as many as possible. And I think that was just very traumatic for the women who encountered that who hadn't thought that was what going south was about." Some black women recognized that white women had cause to complain; one black female member of SNCC, for example, acknowledged that, even though "Negro girls feel neglected because the white girls get the attention . . . [t]he white girls are misused." In spite of this admission, in general, black women did not understand their white sisters' claims of sex discrimination. Some black women blamed white women's low status in the movement on their incompetence; instead of demanding independence, they argued, white women could have worked harder to prove their skills and abilities.

To expose the problems within SNCC, Mary King and Casey Hayden, two longtime white staffers, wrote a position paper protesting discrimination against women; borrowing the language of black oppression, they asserted that "the average SNCC worker finds it difficult to discuss the woman problem because of the assumption of male superiority. Assumptions of male superiority are as widespread and deep-rooted and as crippling to the woman as the assumptions of white supremacy are to the Negro." Delivered anonymously at a SNCC conference in November 1964, King and Hayden's paper provoked derision and little debate; perhaps responding more to women's sexual activity that summer than to the content of the paper, Stokely Carmichael, a future chair of SNCC, quipped that the "position of women in SNCC is prone."

In spite of this dismissive response, King and Hayden's paper set off shock waves that reverberated through social protest movements in the next couple of years. Revising their paper a year later, King and Hayden sent it to forty female activists in SDS, the National Student Association, the Northern Student Movement, and the Student Peace Union. Titled "A Kind of Memo," King and Hayden's paper enumerated women's grievances but concluded that "the chances seem nil that we could start a movement based on anything as distant to general American thought as a sex-caste system." Inspired by the paper, women at an SDS conference in December 1965 walked out from the general meeting and created a separate "Women's Caucus" to discuss women's status in the New Left. At the National Conference for a New Politics, a meeting in August 1967 of virtually every group associated with the New Left, women called for civil rights for their sex. Among the women present were Jo Freeman, a Berkeley graduate who had been a member of the Free Speech Movement and a field worker with the Southern Christian Leadership Conference, and Shulamith Firestone, an art student who had done some activist work with a socialist Zionist group. When the general meeting refused to discuss the resolution the women had written, Freeman and Firestone wrote another, more searing one, asking the conference "to condemn the media for stereotyping women as sex objects, to endorse the revamping of marriage, divorce, and property laws, to support the dissemination of birth control information to all women and the removal of all prohibitions against abortion." When the new resolution also was not discussed, Freeman and Firestone protested, and the meeting's chair told Firestone, "Move on, little girl; we have more important issues to talk about here than women's liberation."

Propelled by a snub that encapsulated the New Left's dismissal of their concerns, Freeman invited a group of women, including Firestone, to meet at her apartment to discuss the status of women. Calling themselves the West Side Group in honor of the location of Freeman's apartment in Chicago, the women talked about everything from their sense of exclusion from the New Left to their fear of speaking in public to their sexuality. To communicate their ideas with the rest of the country, they published a newsletter, *Voice of the Women's Liberation Movement,* which eventually had eight hundred subscribers nationwide.

While the West Side Group was likely the first women's liberation group in the country, other groups quickly sprang up, mainly in large cities or college towns, as young, mainly white, middle-class, college-educated women heard about the movement. When Shulamith Firestone moved to New York in late 1967, she joined the civil rights activist Pam Allen to form New York Radical Women (NYRW), a group with members such as Anne Koedt, who would write the important essay "The Myth of the Vaginal Orgasm"; Kathie Amatniek, who had worked with SNCC during Freedom Summer and who would change her last name to Sarachild to honor her mother; and Carol Hanisch, a civil rights worker with the Southern Conference Education Fund. The group's first action occurred at a Vietnam War protest in Washington DC sponsored by Women Strike for Peace (WSP), a women's peace organization composed of middle-class women who used their status as wives and mothers as a central argument in their opposition to war. On January 15, 1968, members of the West Side Group and New York Radical Women joined the peace protesters, who called themselves the Jeannette Rankin Brigade in memory of the congresswoman from Montana who had voted against the nation's entry in both world wars. The women's liberationists didn't blend in with the crowd, however; about thirty members of NYRW carried a papier-mâché coffin emblazoned with a streamer reading THE BURIAL OF TRADITIONAL WOMANHOOD. At a meeting of women's liberationists and the Rankin Brigade immediately after the march, NYRW critiqued the strikers' compliance with cultural norms of femininity; this critique did not sit well with the older peace activists, many of whom thought that the younger women had disregarded the significance of the war protest. Also offended were some members of the West Side Group, who wanted to demonstrate against the war, not against femininity.

After the Washington protest, NYRW continued to meet, ultimately moving its meetings to the offices of the Southern Conference Education Fund, where twenty or thirty women assembled every week. Although mainly young, middle class, educated, and white, these women had an array of identities and vocations; one was an architect, one was a film editor, and many were artists, journalists, and students. The women

Women and Their Bodies

One of the most successful examples of cooperative feminist work is the Boston Women's Health Book Collective, which produced the now-classic *Our Bodies, Ourselves* in 1970. The book emerged organically from a series of conversations and workshops. At a session on "Women and Their Bodies" at a women's liberation conference in Boston in 1969, women shared stories of the patronizing medical establishment as well as information about pregnancy and birth, contraception, abortion, and orgasm. The organizer of the session, Miriam Hawley, told the crowd of the sexist remark made by her obstetrician after delivering her second child: "He said that he was going to sew me up real tight so there would be more sexual pleasure for my husband." Attendees felt a rush of freedom as they found a space to open up about issues that had always seemed private, even humiliating.

After the conference, some women continued to meet, deciding to research various health-related topics and write papers they would read to the group. In the fall of 1969, wanting to share their new knowledge with the community, they offered a twelve-session course called Women and Their Bodies. They also began revising their papers into a 136-page book they published through a local leftist press. The first printing of five thousand copies sold out almost immediately. And even though the book was reprinted ten times in the next two years, demand for what was initially called *Women and Their Bodies* and later named *Our Bodies, Ourselves* continued to be great, especially since it was handed out at birth control clinics and women's centers. In the fall of 1972, members of the collective incorporated as a nonprofit and signed a contract with Simon and Schuster, which published the enlarged book in 1973.

The publication of *Our Bodies, Ourselves* coincided with and helped to launch the women's health movement that sprang up in the 1970s. The book taught—and continues to teach—countless women about topics as wide-ranging as sexuality, postpartum depression, and the healthcare establishment.

spent much of their time together talking about and analyzing their experiences as women, which, they believed, would lead to personal transformation and then to political action. This practice—termed "consciousness-raising" (or CR) by Kathie Sarachild, perhaps the method's most ardent promoter—allegedly began when NYRW member Anne Forer, unclear about how women were oppressed as a sex, asked members to go around the room describing how they felt burdened as women. In a typical CR session, a small group of women, anywhere from a handful to a dozen, would gather and respond to a particular question. Some groups tried to reconstruct in chronological order their childhood, adolescent, and adult understandings of gender role stereotyping. Other groups examined a wide range of questions about everything from body image and beauty standards to dating and marriage to sexual orientation. Typical questions might be "Do you ever have sex when you don't want to?" "What do you like or dislike about your appearance?" and "Do women have to sacrifice more to make a marriage work?" As they heard multiple responses to a question, women started to see patterns emerging; they began to develop theory as they realized that the problems they had thought were theirs alone were shared by many. From this insight NYRW member Carol Hanisch coined the slogan "the personal is political," which meant that the private arenas of home, marriage, and family reflected the power dynamics of society at large.

Initially the province of radical feminists, CR drew criticism from liberal feminists, who thought its personal emphasis would lead to no social change—indeed, Betty Friedan referred to the practice as "navel-gazing"—and leftists, who thought that, instead of deriving theory from experience, radical women should be reading and debating the ideas of political theorists. In "The Personal Is Political," an essay Hanisch wrote in February 1969 and that appeared in NYRW's *Notes from the Second Year* in 1970, she defended the practice of CR, asserting, "One of the first things we discover in these [consciousness-raising] groups is that personal problems are political problems. There are no personal solutions at this time. There is only collective action for a collective solution." In the mid-1970s, Sarachild defended CR against the criticism that it was merely therapy: "The importance of listening to a woman's feelings was collectively to analyze the situation of women, not analyze her. . . . It was and is the conditions women face, it's male supremacy, we want to change." Other members of women's liberation recognized—perhaps too late—that CR relied too much on generalization and thus excluded women of color from its theories; for instance, Ellen Willis, a member of NYRW and the rock critic for the *New Yorker,* wrote, "[W]e were acting on the unconscious racist assumption that our experience was representative, along with the impulse to gloss over racial specificities so as to keep the 'complication of racism' from marring our vision of female unity."

Like Willis, other radical feminists recognized that they were not speaking for all women. At a small conference held in Sandy Springs, Maryland, in August 1968, women debated whether they should ask Kathleen Cleaver, the communications secretary of the Black Panther Party and the wife of Eldridge Cleaver, for the names of radical black women to invite to an upcoming conference. While some women liked the idea of reaching out to black women, others worried either that black women would not come if invited or that they would not be sympathetic to white women's grievances. As one woman put it, "I don't want to go to a conference and hear a black militant woman tell me she is more oppressed and what am I going to do about it." White women were reluctant to approach women involved with the black power movement because these women tended to understand male–female relationships as traditional, with black females assuming subordinate roles so that black males could take on the dominant ones they were denied in the larger society. Although some women realized that women's liberation would benefit from the inclusion of black women's voices and experiences, no one ever contacted Cleaver, and women's liberation lost a valuable opportunity for interracial dialogue.

Without the input of women of color, women's liberation began to define its agenda. When Carol Hanisch had the idea to protest the Miss America Pageant, NYRW did consciousness-raising and discovered that everyone in the group felt strongly about the beauty standards that American society imposed on women. The zap action, or striking public demonstration, that they planned—a protest in Atlantic City, New Jersey, on September 7, 1968—garnered publicity for the fledgling women's liberation movement. In Atlantic City, two hundred activists marched, carrying signs that read No More Miss America, Can Makeup Cover the Wounds of Our Oppression? If You Want Meat, Go to a Butcher, and The Real Miss America Lives in Harlem. This last sign was certainly a dig at the pageant's racism; until 1940, contestants had to be white, and as of 1968, no black woman had competed in, much less won, the contest. At the protest, one woman auctioned off an oversize Miss America puppet, while others crowned a live sheep Miss America and marched with it

© The Associated Press

Protesters at the Miss America pageant in Atlantic City, New Jersey, September 7, 1968.

down the boardwalk. Protesters threw "objects of female torture"—copies of magazines such as *Ladies' Home Journal* and *Cosmopolitan* as well as false eyelashes, makeup, hair curlers, high-heeled shoes, girdles, and bras—into what they dubbed a "Freedom Trash Can." Although newspapers reported that the protesters burned their bras, such claims were false. Even so, the association between a feminist and a bra burner—or someone opposed to the trappings of conventional femininity—has stuck, even almost fifty years later. Some activists bought tickets to the pageant and, sitting in the balcony of the Convention Hall, unfurled a banner that read WOMEN'S LIBERATION. Other activists inside the hall set off stink bombs; one protester was arrested. All of these actions attempted to convey a rejection of what Robin Morgan, the protest's key organizer, called "the degrading mindless-boob-girlie symbol" pervasive in the media. Newspapers covered the story derisively: In a *New York Post* column written several days after the protest, Harriet Van Horne explained that she did not participate in the event because "this lady of the press usually has something nicer to do on Saturday night than burn her undergarments on the boardwalk in Atlantic City. And I suspect the deep-down aching trouble with these lassies is that they haven't." Even if it covered the story negatively, the media brought the Miss America protest to the nation's attention, and this publicity spurred more women to join NYRW and other women's liberation groups around the country.

As more women joined the movement, conflict within small groups escalated. Disagreement emerged about the relationship between women's liberation and the New Left. Some women, referred to as politicos, felt great connection to the tradition of leftist political analysis and protest; seeing their work as part of a larger leftist project opposed to capitalism, consumerism, advertising, the media, and the war in Vietnam, they did not want to sever their ties to the New Left. Others thought it imperative to dissolve their connection to the Left so they could concentrate on a feminist political analysis and develop an autonomous women's movement. Some women—usually politicos—thought that women's liberation did too much consciousness-raising;

they argued that an overemphasis on discussion meant that they performed too little activism. A final conflict concerned leadership: The small-group format of women's liberation was nonhierarchical and premised on cooperation and collaboration. Eschewing leaders, members of women's liberation did not like to see one woman gain too much media attention or become a movement spokesperson. Women presumed to be seeking the spotlight were labeled as "elitist" or self-promoting; even when a woman was particularly talented as a speaker or a writer, group members clamored for her to step aside to give another woman a chance. At meetings, Kathie Sarachild and Shulamith Firestone were criticized for dominating the conversation; people were troubled when Robin Morgan and, later, Gloria Steinem were anointed movement spokespeople by the media; and when Kate Millett published *Sexual Politics,* a book that landed her on the cover of *Time* magazine, her peers in women's liberation blamed her for seeking the limelight.

Because the many women who flooded the meetings of NYRW after the Miss America protest brought with them divisiveness and conflict, the group broke into a number of smaller factions. One of these groups, Redstockings, was founded by Shulamith Firestone and Ellen Willis. For its first action, Redstockings attended—and disrupted—a public meeting held to debate the reform of abortion law in New York state. On February 13, 1969, members of Redstockings picketed a legislative hearing to which fourteen men and one woman—a nun— had been invited as expert witnesses. When one expert suggested that abortion should be legal for women who had "done their social duty" by bearing four children, Kathie Sarachild interjected, "Alright, now let's hear from some *real* experts—the women!" Other women joined in, demanding that their viewpoint be heard; the meeting broke up shortly thereafter, with the committee members and witnesses moving to another room to continue conferring in private. Inspired by the press coverage of their protest, Redstockings decided to hold a speak-out called "Abortion: Tell It Like It Is" on March 21, 1969. Instead of talking about abortion in abstract, theoretical, or legalistic terms, the organizers of the event decided to use personal testimony, thereby making the issue more concrete for listeners. Members of Redstockings found a dozen women who were willing to speak publicly about their abortions. Just as former slaves speaking on the antislavery circuit in the nineteenth century shared true stories of abuse that convinced their audiences that slavery should be abolished, the courageous women who told complete strangers the often-humiliating details of their painful, private suffering persuaded people that abortion should be legalized. In today's world of television talk shows and online blogging, asking women to tell personal stories may seem an obvious decision, but doing so in the late 1960s broke with the convention that women did not talk publicly about private issues such as sexuality, abortion, or domestic violence; these issues were unmentionable and shameful. Indeed, some of the most uncomfortable and difficult issues—such as whether to have an abortion and, if so, how to find someone to perform the procedure and how to come up with the money to pay for it—were those that women shared with no one, not even their best friends, sisters, or mothers. The decision to have a speak-out turned out to be brilliant; according to Ellen Willis, for the three hundred people in the audience, the personal testimony "evoke[d] strong reactions . . . empathy, anger, pain." Just as protesters of the Vietnam War used the teach-in, women's liberationists saw the speak-out, with its reliance on personal voices, as a way to sway public opinion.

Redstockings was not the only group challenging restrictions to abortion. Formed at a conference on abortion laws in February 1969, the National Association for the Repeal of Abortion Laws (NARAL) asserted its dedication "to the elimination of all laws and practices that would compel any woman to bear a child against her will. To that end, it proposes to initiate and co-ordinate political, social, and legal action of individuals and groups concerned with providing safe operations by qualified physicians for all women seeking them regardless of economic status." Although its name has changed a number of times—it is now called NARAL Pro-Choice America—the group has been advocating for abortion rights longer than any other organization in the United States.

The work of Redstockings and NARAL was forward looking: In 1971, the Supreme Court heard arguments in the *Roe v. Wade* case. On January 22, 1973, the court handed down its decision: A woman's "right of personal privacy includes the abortion decision." Although the court's ruling was important because it offered constitutional protection for a woman's private choice about abortion, the court's majority did not state that "a woman's right is absolute and that she is entitled to terminate her pregnancy as she chooses." That is, *Roe* represented conditional support for abortion—it did not legalize "abortion on demand" as feminists had wanted and instead placed limits on abortion based on the fetus's viability outside the womb. These conditions would open up a space for restrictions on abortion, restrictions that began to be put in place as forces of backlash mobilized in the late 1970s and, especially, in the 1980s.

In addition to giving women a chance to discuss their experiences with abortion, women's liberation allowed women to talk about the way sexual violence altered their lives. At a speak-out organized by NYRW offshoot New York Radical Feminists (NYRF) in January 1971 and attended by more than three hundred women, thirty women described the sexual violence they had experienced. One of the event's organizers was Susan Brownmiller, a thirty-five-year-old journalist and activist who had worked in the civil rights movement, volunteering for Freedom Summer in 1964. Brownmiller explains that, in the early 1970s and before, the "prevailing opinion . . . held that rape was a murky, deviant crime any alert woman could avoid." In most people's minds, rape occurred when a strange man jumped out of the bushes or pulled a woman into an alley; people did not realize that the majority of rapes are committed by men who know their victims. As with the issue of abortion, a culture of silence surrounded the issue of sexual violence, which included not just rape but also domestic violence, which was seen both as a private matter between husband and wife and as something a woman probably provoked. From the stories that emerged at the speak-out, however, women learned that they should not be blamed for sexual violence against them and that sexual assault was about power and domination. After the speak-out in April, NYRF organized a conference on rape, one with a more academic focus. Inspired by what she learned at both events, Brownmiller spent the next four years writing the groundbreaking book *Against Our Will: Men, Women, and Rape,* which was published in 1975.

From all of these discussions of sexual violence, a movement to end violence against women started to take shape. After the establishment of the first rape crisis hotline in Washington DC in 1972, rape crisis centers appeared nationwide, providing advice and support for victims as well as training for people in healthcare and law enforcement. And, although the first shelter for battered women opened in Pasadena, California, in 1964, it wasn't until the 1970s that the idea caught on across the country, with more shelters opening as the decade progressed.

In addition to organizing speak-outs, women's liberationists, regardless of the groups to which they belonged, embarked on a series of actions and protests. These actions led both to publicity for women's liberation and to disagreement within the movement about ideology and motivation. For its inaugural action, members of Women's International Terrorist Conspiracy from Hell (WITCH), another group that splintered off from NYRW, dressed up as witches and put a hex on Wall Street on Halloween 1968. A few months later, in February 1969, WITCH protested a bridal fair held at New York's Madison Square Garden. Wearing black veils and singing, "Here come the slaves, off to their graves," WITCH members held signs saying ALWAYS A BRIDE, NEVER A PERSON and released white mice into the crowd. On September 23, 1969, members of The Feminists (formerly the October 17th Movement) protested at the Marriage License Bureau, charging officials of "committing fraud with malicious intent on the women of New York."

It's not surprising that so many protests centered on marriage: Many radical feminists criticized the institution for making women dependent and subordinate. Many feminists, young women themselves, thought about the compromised lives their mothers had led and didn't want to follow in their footsteps. Motherhood usually followed marriage, and radical feminists objected to the unpaid, low-status work of domesticity. While Pat Mainardi, the author of "The Politics of Housework" and a member of Redstockings, did not reject marriage, she did question men's supremacy and the ironclad sex roles promoted by marriage. Ti-Grace Atkinson saw marriage as detrimental to female solidarity. In her view, because married women are always on some level identifying with men, they can never see themselves "as a member of the class of women." Even if they agreed with such critiques of marriage, other radical feminists criticized the actions directed against marriage for their hostility toward nonmovement women. According to critics, members of WITCH and The Feminists seemed to accuse women of ignorance and false consciousness; because they pointed fingers at allegedly less enlightened women, they actually did more to alienate women than to show sisterhood with them.

When members of Redstockings, The Feminists, and New York Radical Feminists staged a sit-in at the offices of the *Ladies' Home Journal* in March 1970, the results were also mixed. The one hundred to two hundred protesters presented John Mack Carter, the magazine's editor-in-chief, with a list of fourteen demands, including his replacement by a woman, the creation of an onsite cooperative childcare facility, the elimination of ads degrading to women, and the publication of an issue about women's liberation. Initially refusing to capitulate, Carter agreed to negotiate when Shulamith Firestone climbed onto his desk and started to shred copies of the magazine. A group of women met with Carter, who agreed to publish an eight-page insert on women's liberation, paying the women $10,000 for their work. In spite of this concession, some radical feminists thought the action a failure since Carter agreed to so few of their demands and, more seriously, because some women used the action as an opportunity to talk their way into freelance writing gigs. These women, claimed critics, privileged their individual, career-oriented goals over the ideals of the protest itself.

Disagreements such as these about the goals of feminist actions are not surprising given the different priorities and backgrounds of

Feminism at the Newsstand

When *Ms.* magazine began publishing in 1972, most monthly magazines aimed at women focused on beauty and fashion or homemaking and decorating. Most publications directed at feminists were mimeographed articles and newsletters distributed in very small quantities. Created by journalist Gloria Steinem and editor Patricia Carbine, *Ms.* tried to combine the political analysis of feminist publications with the slick production values of women's magazines, becoming in the process the first mainstream feminist periodical on the market.

Appearing inside the December 20, 1971, issue of *New York* magazine, the preview edition of *Ms.* featured articles such as "Raising Kids Without Sex Roles," "Women Tell the Truth About Their Abortions," and "Lesbian Love and Sexuality." Jane O'Reilly's "The Housewife's Moment of Truth" introduced the concept of the "click" to feminist discourse; O'Reilly described the click as the moment of awareness that women feel when they suddenly realize the sexist assumptions permeating their everyday lives. Judy Syfer's now-classic "I Want a Wife" outlined, with great humor, the invisible and unrewarded work done by housewives.

When the first freestanding issue of *Ms.* hit newsstands in July 1972, it sold three hundred thousand copies in eight days. While naysayers such as the television journalist Harry Reasoner quipped that the magazine would last six months before it "ran out of things to say," this prediction proved incorrect: *Ms.* continues to be published more than forty years later. Also critical of the magazine were radical feminists, who saw the publication as offering a watered-down version of women's liberation, one that tried to be palatable and politically correct to everyone. They criticized the glib feminism *Ms.* packaged and delivered along with advertisements that signaled the magazine's co-optation by capitalism. Recognizing that it would not be able to please everyone, *Ms.* tried to find a middle ground that would reach seasoned feminists as well as converts. The many letters it received attested to the magazine's ability to influence and inspire housewives and working women alike. And the periodical's introduction of the word "Ms." to the popular lexicon gave women a title that hid their marital status, analogous to "Mr.," which men had been using for centuries.

second wave feminists. Yet, perhaps more permanently damaging to women's liberation were the rifts created because radical feminists, focused on showing the oppression of women as a "sex class," often failed to think through the ways that differences among women— such as those connected to race and sexuality—mattered a great deal. Many women of color, in particular, tried to distance themselves from radical feminism, stating that feminists were "spoiled," "man-hating," and "wrong in the way they are protesting." Because they saw their race as the primary source of their identity and oppression, many identified with the black nationalist movement rather than with feminism or else thought feminism was unrelated to their lives. For example, the poet Nikki Giovanni wanted no part of the mainstream women's movement, stating that she didn't wish to join a "white family quarrel." In *Woman Power: The Movement for Women's Liberation,* the black writer Celestine Ware described the distance between white and black women, a distance based on different lived experiences. However, Ware seemed to believe in the possibility of interracial cooperation: "Black and white women can work together for women's liberation, but only if the movement changes its priorities to work on issues that affect the lives of minority-group women." Yet, some black women expressed frustration with the allegedly collaborative tactics displayed by white women. One black woman wrote about the "ingratiation and patronage" she had experienced at meetings when white women made "statements of the we're-so-happy-that-ONE-OF-YOU-could-make-it type." Other women of color who self-identified as feminists critiqued white feminists for their narrow vision. In 1979, the poet Audre Lorde condemned the "arrogance" of the organizers of an academic conference for not "examining our many differences" and for not soliciting "significant input from poor women, black and third-world women, and lesbians."

There were women of color, however, who claimed a new kind of feminism for themselves. Although short-lived, the National Black Feminist Organization (NBFO), which formed in 1973, created a space to understand "the vital and revolutionary importance of [feminism] to Third World women, especially black women." The organization sought to focus on the concerns of black women as well as to strengthen the women's movement by informing black women about what feminism really is. In 1974, black lesbians from the NBFO created the Combahee River Collective, a socialist black feminist organization that emphasized the intersections of racial, gender, heterosexual, and class oppression; one of the collective's leaders was Barbara Smith, a writer and critic who would go on to found, with Audre Lorde, Kitchen Table/Women of Color Press, the first publishing house in the United States for women of color. Named after a guerrilla action led by Harriet Tubman during the Civil War, the Combahee River Collective claimed in its mission statement, "[W]e are actively committed to struggling against racial, sexual, heterosexual, and class oppression and see as our particular task the development of integrated analysis and practice based upon the fact that the major systems of oppression are interlocking. The synthesis of these oppressions creates the conditions of our lives." The assertion that oppressions interconnect was a theoretical breakthrough for second wave feminists. The feminism of

© JEB (Joan E. Biren)

Barbara Smith, Audre Lorde, Cherríe Moraga, and Hattie Gossett promoting Kitchen Table/Women of Color Press in 1981.

third world women of color would push this insight further, and third wave feminists in the 1990s would use this analysis to ground their own discussions of oppression.

Another damaging split in the second wave concerned lesbianism, and this schism affected liberal and radical feminists alike. When radical feminist groups began to form in 1967, lesbianism was still considered illicit and taboo; lesbians who wanted to be part of women's liberation felt the need to hide their sexuality. Although there had been lesbian organizations since at least 1955, when Del Martin and Phyllis Lyon formed the Daughters of Bilitis, such groups operated in a covert way, not announcing their presence explicitly. However, once the gay liberation movement began to take shape after the Stonewall riots in 1969, some lesbians began to feel more comfortable asserting their sexual orientation publicly. Feminist groups seemed a natural place to express these feelings; in some groups, such as DC Women's Liberation, New Left activist Marilyn Webb recalls, "we were putting our energy into each other and slowly falling in love with each other as well." In other groups, though, lesbian feminists felt excluded; this was especially apparent in NOW. Rita Mae Brown, a dynamic lesbian feminist who would go on to have much success as the author of the novel *Rubyfruit Jungle,* resigned from her positions in the New York NOW chapter after her many efforts to bring up the issue of sexual orientation were "dismissed as unimportant, too dangerous to contemplate." Worried that the women's movement would be ignored because of its association with homosexuality, Betty Friedan in 1969 labeled lesbianism a "lavender menace," which, if taken seriously, threatened to derail NOW's projects.

After leaving NOW, Brown formed a group called Radicalesbians, which staged a significant action at the Second Congress to Unite Women on May 1, 1970. On the opening night of the conference, Radicalesbians, wearing T-shirts stenciled LAVENDER MENACE, made their way onstage and began explaining the oppression lesbians experienced in a homophobic society. They also distributed copies of "The Woman-Identified Woman," the position paper they had prepared for the event. In the essay, they asserted that lesbianism was a political act, a way of showing solidarity with other women by living with them and without men. Only by creating intimate relationships with women could feminists hope to gain freedom and happiness. The Radicalesbians' action and position paper inspired many women to seek out lesbian relationships or to act on feelings they had been suppressing. Other women saw lesbianism within a purely political context, agreeing with Ginny Berson, who wrote in 1972 that "lesbianism is not a matter of sexual preference, but rather one of political choice which every woman must make if she is to become woman-identified and thereby end male supremacy."

While the Radicalesbians' intentions were quite serious, they staged their action play- fully as a way to educate the women in the audience that lesbianism was a feminist is- sue. Even though the crowd responded in a largely positive manner, a brief piece in *Time* later that year revealing Kate Millett's bisexuality prompted Ti-Grace Atkinson, Gloria Steinem, Susan Brownmiller, and Flo Kennedy to hold a press conference to show support for Millett. At the meeting, they explained that women's lib- eration and gay liberation were

Radicalesbians founder Rita Mae Brown at the Second Congress to Unite Women, 1970.

both "struggling toward a common goal" of not being defined by sex or sexual orientation. For the liberal feminists of NOW, however, alliance with lesbians was still not on the agenda; indeed, Friedan led a purge of the New York NOW chapter, ridding it of lesbians and lesbian sympathizers. Only in 1971 did the organization adopt a resolution supporting an individual's right to define her sexuality as she chose and recognizing the oppression of lesbians. Although this resolution helped the organization to stop thinking oppositionally of the divisions between heterosexual and homosexual feminists, in radical feminist camps, a palpable gay-straight split could be felt: Some small CR groups in large cities never survived this split, and some groups—such as the Furies, a lesbian feminist collective in Washington DC—insisted on the need for lesbians to separate from the feminist majority. Rita Mae Brown, one of the founders of the Furies, explained the appeal of separatism as follows: "A woman can best find out who she is with other women, not with just one other woman but with other women who are also struggling to free themselves from an alien and destructive culture. It is this new concept, that of women-identified women, that sounds the death knell for the male culture and calls for a new culture where cooperation, life and love are the guiding forces of organization rather than competition, power and bloodshed."

As the gay-straight split began to devastate women's liberation in the early 1970s, other versions of feminism started to become popular. Socialist-feminist groups emerged out of the New Left and sought to combine critiques of economic inequality and male supremacy. Like radical feminists, socialist feminists wanted to dismantle a social system based on inequality; unlike radical feminists, socialist feminists were unwilling to name sex as the major cause of women's oppression. Instead, they wanted to establish new systems that would redistribute resources in an equal fashion. Unlike other kinds of feminism, socialist feminism prioritized the needs of poor and working-class women, developing practical programs for their benefit. For instance, members of socialist-feminist groups in New York City created the Committee for Abortion Rights and Against Sterilization Abuse (CARASA), which succeeded in getting the United States Department of Health, Education and Welfare to institute guidelines that would ensure women's consent to sterilization. Bread and Roses, one of

DIY Abortion

Before the Supreme Court handed down its ruling in *Roe v. Wade*, what did women who wanted an abortion do? In rare cases, a woman could get a therapeutic abortion—mainly if a committee of doctors decided that her life was jeopardized by the pregnancy. Women with the means to do so flew to places such as Puerto Rico, Cuba, or London, where a doctor could perform the procedure. Most women found an abortion provider through the grapevine, resorting to "back-alley" procedures with practitioners of questionable credentials. In so doing, they risked their lives and their health to infection or a punctured uterus. Many women tried to induce abortion themselves. Those advocating reform of abortion laws estimated that five thousand women died each year from illegal abortions; the majority of these fatalities resulted from self-induced abortions.

Women in Chicago came up with a different solution for women desperate to abort. In 1969, they created the Jane collective, initially an abortion-referral service. Members of Jane hung posters that stated PREGNANT? DON'T WANT TO BE? CALL JANE AT 643-3844. A "Call-Back Jane" would listen to the message recorded by an abortion seeker, visit her, and schedule an appointment with a provider the group had already screened.

Beginning in 1971, after one "Jane" learned the technique from a provider, members of the collective began to perform abortions themselves. This Jane taught others in the group how to use clamps, curettes, and forceps to perform the procedure. Because so many women became skilled at it, the collective performed about thirty abortions a day, charging rates that were much more reasonable than those on offer on the black market. They continued this work until May 3, 1972, when the group was caught. Seven women were arrested, but all of the charges against them were ultimately dropped after the Supreme Court's *Roe* decision was announced in early 1973.

the most famous socialist-feminist groups, began in Boston in 1969 and had a wide range of activities, including organizing pink-collar workers and high school students. Founded in the same year, the Chicago Women's Liberation Union (CWLU) had an even bigger agenda; among many other things, it helped women in prison, ran a legal clinic, and created Jane, an abortion-referral service. The heyday of socialist feminism ended in the mid-1970s.

Another variant of feminism was cultural feminism, which advocated a "women's culture" of art, music, and women-created institutions and found an audience among people tired of the factionalism of radical feminism. Because it valued the female in ways that radical feminists had not—holding up nurturance and cooperation as well as love of the environment and peace as essential, "female" qualities and goals— cultural feminism appealed to a wide range of women, some of whom were less interested in formal activism than in a lifestyle that embraced women's music festivals, such as the Michigan Womyn's Music Festival; businesses run by women, such as Olivia Records; and publications written and edited by women, such as *Quest: A Feminist Quarterly.* Because of their focus on women's experiences, the institutions created by cultural feminists offered, in Robin Morgan's words, "concrete moves toward self-determination and power for women." Deriving support from a lesbian community activated by both the gay liberation and the women's liberation movements, cultural feminism sometimes advocated the kind of separatism found in lesbian feminist collectives. As a result of this separatism and its emphasis on culture as opposed to activism, some contemporary feminists—liberal and radical alike—critiqued cultural feminism. Betty Friedan saw cultural feminism as "a schizophrenic retreat from the necessities and actual possibilities of the modern women's movement." Brooke Williams, a radical feminist, claimed that cultural feminism could "transform feminism from a political movement to a lifestyle movement." Ellen Willis was perhaps the harshest in her assessment, stating that, instead of "a radical feminist analysis of women's concrete, material oppression [cultural feminists] substitute fantasies of lost matriarchies, female superiority and 'mother right.'"

Even as the rise of cultural feminism began to signal the end of the radical wing of the women's movement, feminism as a mass movement began to make a noticeable impact on American society. Thanks to *Ms.* magazine, which published a guide to consciousness-raising in 1973, and NOW, whose individual chapters began to create CR groups for interested members, more women used small-group dialogue to explore their status as women. Events such as the Women's Strike for Equality in 1970 transmitted a feminist message that was neither liberal nor radical in nature. As the decade progressed, issue-oriented groups and organizations—rape crisis centers, women's shelters, and women's health centers, for example—sprang up and institutionalized some of the causes and issues radical feminists had helped to theorize and publicize. Gains made by feminists in the 1970s led to a more equitable educational arena for women. The passage of Title IX of the Higher Education Act in 1972 prohibited sex discrimination in schools receiving federal funding. In practical terms, Title IX opened up athletics to girls and young women, since institutions were required to provide funding and opportunities to female students. As a result of the legislation, parents demanded that school boards and local Little Leagues include girls in their sports programming. At the college level, female students participated in sports in growing numbers: Before Title IX, about sixteen thousand played college sports; by 1984, nearly ten times that many women were college athletes. Fearing that it would mean fewer opportunities for male athletes, the National Collegiate Athletics Association (NCAA) fought against Title IX and succeeded at slowing its enforcement; by the end of the 1970s, no institution had been fined for not complying with the law. Feminists changed the educational landscape off the sports field, as well: In 1974, the passage of the Women's Educational Equity Act meant that federal money could be spent to buy materials and implement programs that challenged sexism. One beneficiary of this legislation was the new field of women's studies, an interdisciplinary academic endeavor aimed at examining gender inequality in social, historical, and cultural terms.

The formation of the National Women's Studies Association in 1977 offered a professional organization to those involved in such academic pursuits.

Crucial to the popularization of feminism in the 1970s was the creation of an important political organization and the planning of a significant conference. In forming the National Women's Political Caucus (NWPC) in 1971, Betty Friedan, Gloria Steinem, and Congresswomen Shirley Chisholm, Bella Abzug, and Patsy Mink sought to involve women in politics to a greater degree than ever before. As Shirley Chisholm explained, "[T]he function of the National Women's Political Caucus is not to be the cutting edge of the women's liberation movement, but the big umbrella organization which provides the weight and the muscle for those issues which the majority of women in this country see as concerns." In addition to encouraging women to enter politics, the bipartisan caucus gained more female delegates to political conventions; brought women's issues, such as access to reproductive rights, the need for affordable childcare, and the desire for the ERA, to the attention of the political parties; and supported candidates—female or male—with feminist agendas. One of the strengths of the NWPC was not just its bipartisanship but its diversity. The national leadership initially included many women of color, such as the Indian rights activist LaDonna Harris; civil rights activists Myrlie Evers and Fannie Lou Hamer; the president of the National Council of Negro Women, Dorothy Height; and NOW president Wilma Scott Heide.

Similarly animated by a strategy of inclusiveness were the International Women's Year Conference held in Houston in 1977 and the statewide conferences leading up to it. For many, these conferences signaled that feminism had become mainstream since they were supported by the federal government: President Jimmy Carter named Bella Abzug to organize the conference, and Congress allocated $5 million to support it. Attending the conference were two thousand delegates representing a wide range of constituencies, as well as eighteen thousand observers. Even if second wave feminism has the reputation of being a movement of white, middle-class women, 35 percent of the delegates to the Houston conference were nonwhite, and 20 percent came from low-income backgrounds. The competing interests of the delegates led to some difficulty in agreeing on the "Plan for Action," the document that outlined the needs of the delegates' constituencies; however, after much debate, the delegates adopted the twenty-six-item agenda, which included support for the ERA, reproductive freedom, and minority and lesbian rights. As one feminist remembered the Houston conference twenty years later, "[W]e women found sisterhood—that universal sense of being together honorably for a great cause. Even now . . . women who don't know each other will find themselves reminiscing about Houston in the same way war veterans, strangers on sight, quickly become close as they talk about Normandy, Inchon, or Hue."

In spite of the Houston conference's energetic support of the ERA, the amendment would fail to gain ratification only five years later; even if only symbolically, this failure signaled the end of second wave feminism, which had been declining in its radical form for almost ten years. When the House of Representatives and the Senate approved the Equal Rights Amendment—in October 1971 and March 1972, respectively—feminists were ecstatic, convinced that, even if it took some time, the ratification of the amendment was a given. They had reason for such optimism: By the end of 1972, twenty-two of the needed thirty-eight states had ratified the amendment. By 1975, however, the ratification process began to slow, and sixteen states had defeated the amendment. And in 1977, nine more states rejected or tabled the amendment. Perhaps even worse, several states rescinded their earlier passage of the amendment, indicating that the tide was turning against the constitutional change. It seemed unlikely that the ERA would be ratified by the 1979 deadline, so feminist organizations such as NOW and the National Women's Political Caucus devoted much energy and money to extending this deadline. Although the groups succeeded at postponing the ratification deadline until 1982, ultimately the ERA was defeated when, in June 1982, North Carolina tabled the amendment and Florida and Illinois rejected it.

The approval of the ERA seemed a certainty in the early 1970s, so what happened? The wording of the ERA, which was revised in 1943 by Alice Paul, seemed innocuous enough, stating: "Equality of rights under the law shall not be denied or abridged by the United States or by any state on account of sex." However, opponents to the amendment worried that the entire fabric of society would be altered by the ERA. Anti-ERA conservatives used various arguments to defeat it. Two that received widespread media attention included the distracting claim that the ERA would mean the rise of unisex bathrooms and the more serious contention that it would lead to the drafting of women into the military. These scare tactics diverted attention from the core meaning of the amendment. Phyllis Schlafly, an antifeminist who managed to organize tremendous opposition to the amendment, played a significant role in the ERA's defeat. Through her monthly newsletter, *The Phyllis Schlafly Report,* her Stop ERA campaign, and the Eagle Forum, a conservative organization she founded, Schlafly communicated her views about the ERA's danger to the American home and family. Schlafly doesn't deserve sole credit for the ERA's failure—feminist activists may not have done enough on the state level to gain the amendment's passage—but she was part of a larger picture coming into focus by 1980: the rise of the New Right, a conservative movement that would put the family and morality at the center of its arguments. As the next chapter will explore, the backlash to feminism launched by right-wing political groups in the 1980s succeeded in both overturning some of the gains made by second wave feminists and creating an atmosphere hostile to further feminist activism.

Chapter 4

Third Wave Feminism: Embracing Contradiction

WHILE IT IS RELATIVELY EASY TO LOCATE the origins of the first and second waves of the women's movement in the United States—we can point to the Seneca Falls Convention in 1848 as the starting point for the first wave and, perhaps more arbitrarily, to the Miss America protest in 1968 for the second—finding a beginning moment for the third wave and talking about its history are more complicated. For one thing, the third wave is occurring right now; it is often hard to see outside of the history we are living. And because the first and second waves have ended, we can organize a narrative of their histories in terms of their achievements, even if those achievements represent only a partial list of the goals of their participants. So, even if first wavers aimed for more than suffrage (and some did), we understand the first wave in terms of its end point—the Nineteenth Amendment. Similarly, even though second wavers attempted to make some radical social and cultural changes, for instance by challenging women's role as childbearers, history remembers the legal victories they gained in terms of women's access to education, jobs, and reproductive choice. In contrast, since the third wave is ongoing, we cannot have a full sense of its accomplishments, and any narrative of its history—since it is contemporary—is incomplete. Most people, however, agree that the third wave began in the early 1990s, in large part as a response to the hostility to feminism represented by the outcome of the Clarence Thomas Supreme Court confirmation hearings. And just as the second wave had a myriad of participants both liberal and radical, third wave feminists work within and against social institutions, aiming both to reform society and to alter its very foundations.

Although second wavers continued to work in women's studies programs, feminist nongovernmental organizations, and the antiviolence movement, the conservative political climate created by the rise of the New Right in the late 1970s along with the decade's weak economy led to conditions hostile to the perpetuation and growth of the feminist movement. In *Backlash: The Undeclared War Against American Women*, Susan Faludi explains that the 1980s witnessed "a powerful counter-assault on women's rights, a backlash, an attempt to retract the handful of small and hard-won victories that the feminist movement did manage to win for women." As part of this backlash, the New Right, represented by groups such as Jerry Falwell's Moral Majority and Phyllis Schlafly's Eagle Forum, aimed to reform American culture, which it believed was in decline as secular values replaced religious ones. Instead of manifesting a concern with economic conservatism, as the Old Right had done, the New Right promoted "family values," which it defined in terms of the traditional patriarchal family headed by a breadwinning father and nurtured by a domestic mother. According to the New Right, feminism repudiated such values; in 1980, the Republican presidential campaign blamed feminists for rising divorce rates, the epidemic of single motherhood, and the increase in welfare recipients. Responding to real changes and perceived threats to more "traditional" gender arrangements, members of the New Right set out to challenge feminists and the policies they promoted. The withdrawal of the Republican Party's support for the ERA in 1980 indicated not just the New Right's dominance of the party, which had supported the ERA for forty years, but also the party's antagonism to feminism.

After the election of Ronald Reagan in 1980, forces of opposition gathered to reverse the gains made by second wave activists. Reagan and his conservative administration cut feminists from commissions and departments in the federal government; the replacements appointed to these positions were typically opposed to affirmative action and other liberal reforms beneficial to women and people of color. In addition, the Reagan administration slashed funding to social service agencies and nonprofits whose policies were liberal in orientation. The most serious challenge to the feminist agenda, however, occurred in the area of abortion rights. As early as 1976, antiabortion groups claimed a victory with the passage of the Hyde Amendment, which prohibited the use of Medicaid funding for abortion services, except in cases of rape and incest or if the mother's life was threatened by the continuation of the pregnancy. As a result of the Hyde Amendment, poor women no longer could afford abortions; indeed, access to abortion became as linked to economic status as it had been in the days before *Roe.* In 1989, in *Webster v. Reproductive Health Services,* the Supreme Court upheld a Missouri law that defined life as beginning at conception and forbade abortions performed by public employees in public facilities. The law also banned any counseling about abortion in these facilities and insisted that doctors perform fetal viability tests at twenty weeks. The *Webster* decision paved the way for states to design more and more restrictive abortion laws, which many did. Although the court's decision three years later in *Planned Parenthood Association of Southeastern Pennsylvania v. Casey* reaffirmed a woman's right to abort a pregnancy, the ruling upheld the Pennsylvania law's requirement that a woman submit to counseling and a twenty-four-hour waiting period before she could have an abortion.

While rulings such as these made abortion less and less available, the protests of antiabortion activists were making it harder both for women to get abortions and for medical staff to provide them. Starting in the late 1970s, radicals within the right-to-life movement targeted clinics where abortions were performed; according to law enforcement records, by 1990 there had been eight bombings, twenty-eight acts of arson, twenty-eight arson or bombing attempts, and 170 acts of vandalism at the nation's abortion clinics. In the 1980s, the antiabortion group Operation Rescue, headed by the evangelical Randall Terry, gained notoriety for its protests at abortion clinics; although the group claimed to use peaceful methods of civil disobedience, members of Operation Rescue intimidated patients seeking access to clinics. The

The Sex Wars

Coinciding with the waning of the second wave, the so-called sex wars of the 1980s led to deep divisions in the feminist movement. Prompted by the release of *Snuff* in 1976, a pornographic film that eroticizes the torture and dismemberment of women, San Franciscans formed Women Against Violence in Pornography and Media; three years later, Women Against Pornography was founded in New York. While these groups identified pornography as a crucial feminist issue in the late 1970s, it wasn't until 1982, when the Scholar and Feminist IX Conference at Barnard College examined the topic "Towards a Politics of Sexuality," that a discussion of female sexuality and pornography became more mainstream, ultimately splitting feminists into factions.

On one side of the debate were those opposed to pornography, sometimes referred to as anti-sex or anti-porn feminists, who believed that porn not only degrades women but also objectifies and dehumanizes them, thereby setting the stage for violence against them. Employing the mantra "pornography is the theory; rape is the practice," anti-porn feminists such as legal scholar Catharine MacKinnon and activist Andrea Dworkin argued that pornography violates women's civil rights; they teamed up to write municipal ordinances against pornography in Minneapolis and Indianapolis. MacKinnon and Dworkin gained notoriety not just for these ordinances but for their analysis of male sexual penetration as a sign of

scare tactics of Operation Rescue grew so extreme that volunteers—many of them young women who had never before been involved in any kind of feminist activism—organized a clinic defense movement to help ensure that women could get the services they needed. Perhaps because of the work of the clinic defenders, by the 1990s antiabortion activists ratcheted up their violence and even resorted to murder: Dr. David Gunn, an abortion provider in Florida, was shot in 1993; Gunn's successor, Dr. John Britton, and his volunteer escort, James Barrett, were killed the following year, as were staff members at two Massachusetts abortion clinics. As a result of restrictions from the courts as well as clinic violence, by 1987, 85 percent of the counties men's ownership of women. Although MacKinnon's and Dworkin's ideas were incorrectly, even reductively, depicted to suggest that all heterosexual sex was akin to rape, anti-sex feminists' hostility to pornography did carry over into their attitude toward sex in general.

On the other side of the debate were pro-sex or anti-censorship feminists, who, even if they did not personally support the pornography industry, felt that to suppress porn would be to deny some their First Amendment rights in order to protect one class of people. Pro-sex feminists wanted to help sex workers, who often suffered from dangerous working conditions, abusive bosses, and the threat of disease. Pro-sex feminists also questioned the way anti-sex feminists aimed to desexualize women by promoting the idea that sex itself is something dangerous and harmful. Central to the values of pro-sex feminists is the idea that female sexuality is something to be embraced and nurtured. Some pro-sex feminists value pornography made to enhance women's sexual pleasure; they argue that porn can lead to women's understanding and ownership of their sexuality. For some theorists, the term "pro-sex feminist," which might seem to convey an unreflective sexual voracity or else doctrinaire opposition to the anti-porn position, is less useful than "sex-positive feminist" or "feminist sex radical." These terms advance the idea that female sexuality must be cultivated, even when it participates in systems of oppression. While exuberant about sexuality, feminist sex radicals also recognize that valuing women's sexuality in a culture that has always supported the sexual double standard is an important political position.

in the United States provided no abortion services at all. In addition, fewer and fewer medical schools were teaching abortion procedures; by 1992, residents in obstetrics and gynecology could learn how to perform abortions in only 12 percent of their programs.

Just as a conservative social and political climate revealed a backlash to feminism, in what would end up being a popular refrain the media declared that women were no longer interested in feminism. Perhaps the first articulation of this claim appeared in Susan Bolotin's "Voices from the Postfeminist Generation," a 1982 *New York Times Magazine* cover story. As Bolotin observed, "[N]ot one woman I spoke to believes that women receive equal pay for equal or comparable work, but it does not occur to most of them to use the power of the feminist movement to improve their position." Instead of relying on collective action, the women interviewed for the article believed that inequality should be addressed on an individual level; as one woman put it, "Sure, there's discrimination out there, but you can't just sit there feeling sorry for yourself. It's the individual woman's responsibility to prove her worth. Then she can demand equal pay."

Although many women in the so-called "postfeminist generation" acknowledged the successes of feminism, claiming that the women's movement made life better for them, few called themselves feminists. In 1986, an article in *Elle* stated that young women "no longer need to examine the whys and hows of sexism. . . . All those ideals that were once held as absolute truths—sexual liberation, the women's movement, true equality—have been debunked or debased." According to Bolotin's article and subsequent pieces on postfeminism, younger women felt alienated by what they perceived as the stridency of angry feminists. When journalist Paula Kamen interviewed young women in the late 1980s, she learned that when they heard the word "feminist," they came up with the following associations: "bra-burning, hairy-legged, amazon, castrating, militant-almost-anti-feminine, communist, Marxist, separatist, female skinheads, female supremacists, he-woman type, bunch-a-lesbians." Believing that feminism was passé and many of its goals accomplished, young women did not want to be labeled feminists because of the negative connotations associated with the word.

As a result of this complex of forces—a backlash to feminism, negative stereotypes of feminists, the idea that feminist activism was outmoded and unnecessary—as well as the almost defeatist mentality that set in after the failure of the ERA, some feminist organizations saw their member rolls shrink; by the mid-1980s, NOW's membership declined from 200,000 to 130,000. Yet, it would be a mistake to believe the reports of feminism's death; as historian Sara Evans and others remind us, feminist activism persisted in the 1980s. One important way feminist work continued—and deepened—was through the writing of women of color. In 1979, the Chicana feminists Cherríe

Moraga and Gloria Anzaldúa asked feminists of color to join them in creating a new anthology; in their request for contributions, they wrote: "We want to express to all women—especially to white middle-class women—the experiences which divide us as feminists; we want to examine incidents of intolerance, prejudice and denial of difference within the feminist movement. We intend to explore the causes and sources of, and solutions to these divisions. We want to create a definition that explains what feminist means to us."

The result of their call for papers was *This Bridge Called My Back: Writings by Radical Women of Color,* a book that not only redefined feminism to include the concerns of women of color and third world women but also called into question traditional ways of understanding knowledge by incorporating a variety of different kinds of writing about gendered identity, such as poetry, consciousness-raising essays, and visual art. *This Bridge Called My Back* proved influential to those who became involved in third wave feminism in the 1990s, as did the writing of people such as Audre Lorde, bell hooks, and Alice Walker. Along with the work of these writers, *All the Women Are White, All the Blacks Are Men, But Some of Us Are Brave,* an anthology edited by Patricia Bell Scott, Gloria T. Hull, and Barbara Smith, developed the field of black feminism, which Walker helped to define by coining and explaining the term "womanism" in her essay collection *In Search of Our Mothers' Gardens: Womanist Prose.*

In addition to this intellectual work, feminist activity continued in other professional arenas as "policy feminists" researched women's issues in think tanks and nongovernmental organizations. Feminists divided into camps, and this division decreased their public visibility as a vibrant movement; policy feminists distanced themselves from the abstract theories of academic feminists and the separatist women's culture advocated by cultural feminists. However, in spite of this fragmentation, women continued to make their voices heard on issues they cared deeply about; for instance, in November 1989, approximately 150,000 protesters marched to the Lincoln Memorial to demonstrate the voting power of the pro-choice movement. All through the 1980s,

Defining Womanism

Womanist. 1. From womanish. *(Opp. of "girlish," i.e., frivolous, irresponsible, not serious.) A black feminist or feminist of color. From the black folk expression of mothers to female children, "You acting womanish," i.e., like a woman. Usually referring to outrageous, audacious, courageous, or* willful *behavior. Wanting to know more and in greater depth than is considered "good" for one. Interested in grown-up doings. Acting grown up. Being grown up. Interchangeable with another black folk expression: "You trying to be grown." Responsible. In charge. Serious.*

2. Also: A woman who loves other women, sexually and/or nonsexually. Appreciates and prefers women's culture, women's emotional flexibility (values tears as natural counterbalance of laughter), and women's strength. Sometimes loves individual men, sexually and/or nonsexually. Committed to survival and wholeness of entire people, male and female. Not a separatist, except periodically, for health. Traditionally universalist, as in: "Mama, why are we brown, pink, and yellow, and our cousins are white, beige, and black?" Ans.: "Well, you know the colored race is just like a flower garden, with every color flower represented." Traditionally capable, as in: "Mama, I'm walking to Canada and I'm taking you and a bunch of other slaves with me." Reply: "It wouldn't be the first time."

women gained visibility in the public arena. In 1981, Sandra Day O'Connor became the first female justice on the Supreme Court. In 1984, Geraldine Ferraro became the first woman nominated for vice president by the Democratic Party. In 1989, the Episcopal Church elected African American Barbara C. Harris as its first female bishop.

Meanwhile, women created and became involved in various kinds of political and activist organizations. Founded in 1985, EMILY's List represented a continuation of the legacy of liberal feminism. In 1982, when Ellen Malcolm, a philanthropist and former press secretary for the National Women's Political Caucus, helped raise $50,000 for Harriet

3. Loves music. Loves dance. Loves the moon. Loves the Spirit. Loves love and food and roundness. Loves struggle. Loves the Folk. Loves herself. Regardless.

4. Womanist is to feminist as purple is to lavender.

Novelist Alice Walker crafted a new term, "womanist," that would help define feminism for women of color, particularly black women. Placed at the front of *In Search of Our Mothers' Gardens: Womanist Prose,* a collection of essays she published in 1983, Walker's definition has generated much conversation and has influenced countless people who have wanted to understand how the feminism of women of color can be characterized.

Perhaps the most controversial part of Walker's definition is the final entry, which offers an analogy: "Womanist is to feminist as purple is to lavender." Some people have interpreted this statement as saying that womanism is superior to feminism, that it is a richer, more vibrant "purple" compared to a somewhat washed-out "lavender." In an interview in 1984, Walker defended her definition, stating, "I don't choose womanism because it is 'better' than feminism. . . . Since womanism *means* black feminism, this would be a nonsensical distinction. I choose it because I prefer the sound, the feel, the fit of it, because I cherish the spirit of the women (like Sojourner) the word calls to mind. . . ."

The new word, which has been used by women of color feminists as well as feminist theologians, helps to illustrate a statement made by Audre Lorde in *Sister Outsider:* "Black feminism is not white feminism in black face." Instead, it is a rich, unique way of thinking based in the traditions of black culture.

Woods, who was running for the U.S. Senate on the Democratic ticket in Missouri, she realized that Woods, an experienced state politician who lost by less than 1 percent of the vote, might have won had she had access to funding earlier in her campaign. From this insight, Malcolm created a feminist political action committee based on the premise that "early money is like yeast" (thus the acronym EMILY); the new organization's goal was to support pro-choice Democratic women by providing them with resources early in their campaigns. Malcolm and the friends she involved in the organization thought that the time was ripe for such a political action committee since women, thanks to second wave feminism, were working outside the home in greater numbers than ever and thus had more resources to support the candidates they wanted to see elected. Because of EMILY's List, which contributed 20 percent of her funding, Barbara Mikulski won her Senate race in 1986; thanks to the political action group, between 1986 and 1990 seven women were elected to the U.S. House of Representatives. And in 1990, EMILY's List funded the successful gubernatorial campaigns of Ann Richards in Texas and Barbara Roberts in Oregon. EMILY's List continues to work to elect progressive women to office today.

A very different kind of organization that was also founded in 1985, the Guerrilla Girls performed activism reminiscent of the zap actions of women's liberation in the late 1960s and early 1970s. Organized by an anonymous group of artists, writers, performers, and filmmakers, the Guerrilla Girls exposed sexism and racism in politics, film, and everyday culture, but they devoted most of their attention to uncovering the art world's discrimination against women and people of color. They staged performances, conducted lectures and workshops, and organized exhibitions highlighting the work of women artists. They were, however, perhaps most well known for their public demonstrations. Dressed in gorilla masks, members of the group distributed flyers and hung posters that raised the public's consciousness about sexism in the art world. A poster from 1985 asked How MANY WOMEN HAD ONE PERSON EXHIBITIONS AT NYC MUSEUMS LAST YEAR? Only one, the poster revealed, at the Museum of Modern Art; the Metropolitan Museum of Art, the Guggenheim, and the Whitney all featured no one-woman exhibits. By 1987, the Guerrilla Girls had achieved some fame: *New York* magazine named them one of the four most influential figures in the contemporary art community, and the New York City chapter of NOW gave them the Susan B. Anthony Award. Frustrated that, in spite of this publicity, the art world wasn't changing quickly enough, in 1989 the Guerrilla Girls issued perhaps their most famous poster, which asked Do WOMEN HAVE TO BE NAKED TO GET INTO THE MET. MUSEUM? As their posters indicate, the Guerrilla Girls made free use of humor to get their message across; as the group, which is still active today, states on its website, humor "gets people involved" and is an "effective weapon" against sexism. It also challenges the idea that, because feminists are angry, they are humorless.

A remake of the Guerrilla Girls's 1989 poster targeting the Metropolitan Museum of Art in New York, this image was placed on sandwich boards and carried around the Shanghai Contemporary Art Fair in September 2007.

Ecofeminism

In many ways a product of second wave thinking, ecofeminism represents a bridge between feminist generations. As its name suggests, ecofeminism merges concerns about the environment with a feminist outlook. Coined in 1974 by Françoise d'Eaubonne, a French feminist, in her essay "Le féminisme ou la mort [Feminism or Death]," the term did not gain popularity in the United States until March 1980, when Ynestra King and other activists organized "Women and Life on Earth," a conference held in Amherst, Massachusetts. In describing how the five hundred women at the conference "explored the meaning of ecofeminism as a force for the future," Carolyn Merchant, an important ecofeminist theorist, explains what the women concluded: "[A]s mothers, nurturers, and caretakers, women should direct their creative energies to heal the planet, bringing to the public sphere the care and concern of women for all of life, and that, as feminists, women should work to transform the institutions of modern society that discriminate against women and minorities."

As interest in ecofeminism expanded in the 1980s, its theoretical and activist components focused on both reclaiming the environment and developing spiritual practices that honored women's deep commitment to the earth and its resources. Many people recognize ecofeminism's debt to cultural feminism, which celebrates women's special status as life-giver

Unlike EMILY's List and the Guerrilla Girls, the activism that developed in the 1980s to protest the treatment of AIDS patients did not focus only on a female constituency. Instead, this activism united the gay community and laid the groundwork for explorations of gender fluidity undertaken by third wavers in the next decade. When the Centers for Disease Control identified it as a new disease in 1981, acquired immune deficiency syndrome (AIDS) was dimly understood. As time progressed, clinicians and researchers learned that the human immunodeficiency virus (HIV), which causes AIDS, spreads through sexual intercourse, blood transfusions, and infected needles. Since the disease was perceived as affecting only them, gay men found themselves more stigmatized than ever during the early years of the AIDS epidemic.

and nurturer; because of this status, argue ecofeminists, women have insight into the patriarchal domination not just of the female sex but of the environment itself. Ecofeminists blame a patriarchal, capitalist economy for devastating the earth's natural resources in its search for profits. To distance themselves from patriarchal society, many ecofeminists are part of the feminist spirituality movement, with its goddess worship and use of pagan rituals.

One of the criticisms of ecofeminism is that it, like cultural feminism, relies on an essentialist understanding of gender. Ynestra King's "The Eco-feminist Imperative" reveals this essentialism: "We believe that a culture against nature is a culture against women. We know we must get out from under the feet of men as they go about their projects of violence. In pursuing these projects men deny and dominate both women and nature. It is time to reconstitute our culture in the name of that nature, and of peace and freedom, and it is women who can show the way." King's formulation invokes essentialist categorizations—after all, not all men are purveyors of violence and not all women are promoters of peace. More recent ecofeminist writings are concerned less with such essentialism than with the way global capitalism's destruction of the environment has reproduced social inequalities so that the rich in developed countries remain rich and the poor of the developing world are cast further into poverty.

To respond to the health crisis of AIDS, in 1987 gay men and lesbians formed the AIDS Coalition to Unleash Power, or ACT UP. The group organized protests and demonstrations to demand more access to experimental drugs as well as a national policy to combat the epidemic. ACT UP made its points dramatically; for instance, on September 14, 1989, seven members of the group chained themselves to a balcony at the New York Stock Exchange to protest the high price of AZT, the only federally approved AIDS drug. The demonstration worked: Several days later, the maker of AZT lowered the drug's price. In January 1988, after *Cosmopolitan* magazine published an article claiming that heterosexual sex posed negligible risk for a woman, even if her male partner were infected with HIV, ACT UP protested the magazine's transmission of erroneous information. Picketing outside the offices of the magazine, 150 members of the group held signs that read YES, THE COSMO GIRL CAN GET AIDS! Although *Cosmopolitan* issued a partial retraction, women in ACT UP realized they needed to work together both to show that women could get AIDS and to ensure that women understood how to protect themselves against the disease. After forming a Women's Caucus, in 1991 these members of ACT UP published *Women, AIDS, and Activism,* the first book about women and AIDS.

The confrontational and direct style of ACT UP succeeded in shaking people up; it showed the public that the gay community would not accept poor healthcare or inadequate information about AIDS. Another activist group, Queer Nation, which began in New York in 1990, sought to protest the rampant homophobia in American culture. Through its use of the slogan "We're here. We're queer. Get used to it," the group called attention to members of the LGBT community who didn't want to be invisible any longer; in the process, the organization also reclaimed the word "queer," which had long been used pejoratively. ACT UP and Queer Nation are significant not just for the content of their activist work but also for the way they were able to bring together members of the queer community; in particular, as the 1980s progressed, lesbians, rejecting a history of separatism, identified with the larger gay community. In addition, the activist work of these groups opened up discussions about sexuality, especially among younger women who would later become involved in the third wave.

As the 1990s began and the Clarence Thomas confirmation hearings gained the media spotlight in October 1991, feminists of all kinds—liberals, radicals, teenagers, college students—rallied around a cause that energized feminist camps and, some say, launched a new wave of the women's movement. When Supreme Court justice Thurgood Marshall announced his retirement in June 1991, President George H. W. Bush nominated Clarence Thomas to serve as only the second African American jurist in the high court's history. Although the replacement of Marshall, a famed civil rights leader, with Thomas, a former head of the EEOC opposed to both affirmative action and comparable worth, disappointed feminists, they did not expect to be able to challenge his appointment in any serious way. However, after the media disclosed that the Senate Judiciary Committee had suppressed information about Thomas's alleged sexual harassment of a female employee, feminist groups, along with Democratic congresswomen, demanded an investigation into the charges. Thomas's accuser was Anita Hill, an African American law professor at the University of Oklahoma, who had worked for Thomas in the early 1980s at both the Department of Education and the EEOC. There, Thomas, who had asked her out repeatedly, allegedly made crude remarks about sex and pornographic films he had seen. During the televised hearings of the all-male Judiciary Committee, members, incredulous about this "sexual harassment crap," questioned Hill aggressively and harshly, asking her for details about Thomas's behavior. Although Thomas denied all allegations and referred to the hearings as a "high-tech lynching," Hill remained composed, even as she was subjected to derision while reliving a part of her past she probably wanted to forget. The investigation into Hill's claims did not lead to the rejection of Thomas's candidacy, however; the Senate narrowly confirmed him with a vote of fifty-two to forty-eight.

The Thomas confirmation hearings have been credited with revitalizing the women's movement, and certainly the growing involvement of women in politics in the year after the hearings bears out this claim. The controversial public investigation of Anita Hill's allegations brought attention to the issue of sexual harassment and the inequalities women face in the workplace. Although most people didn't side with Hill initially—in 1991, public opinion polls showed that 47 percent of those asked believed Thomas, while only 24 percent believed Hill—by 1992 people's perceptions shifted, with 44 percent believing Hill and only 34 percent believing Thomas. In addition to reconsidering their attitudes toward Hill, people identified and took action against the harassment they had experienced at work: Sexual harassment complaints filed with the EEOC more than doubled after the public hearings, going from 6,127 in 1991 to 15,342 in 1996. Perhaps sparked by the controversy, which revealed how women's concerns weren't being heard or understood by an overwhelmingly male Senate, women ran for office in greater numbers than ever before, prompting the media to call 1992 the "Year of the Woman." In the 1992 general election, eleven women ran for the Senate, and five, all Democrats, emerged victorious, including incumbent Barbara Mikulski and newcomers Patty Murray, Barbara Boxer, Dianne Feinstein, and Carol Moseley Braun, the first black female senator ever elected. In the House of Representatives, twenty-four women won new seats.

Younger women were also galvanized by the Thomas–Hill controversy. In January 1992, Rebecca Walker, the daughter of the novelist Alice Walker, published "Becoming the Third Wave" in *Ms.* magazine. In this essay, she explains that the hearings sent a "clear message" to women: "Shut up! Even if you speak, we will not listen." Walker, however, refused silence, stating that she "intend[ed] to fight back," to devote her life to women's empowerment. Walker ends her short article with a "plea" to the women of her generation, asking them to remember that "the fight is far from over" and that they should not associate with men—as lovers, friends, or elected officials—"if they don't prioritize our freedom to control our bodies and our lives." Walker's final sentences boldly declare: "I am not a postfeminism feminist. I am the Third Wave." Walker's reclamation of feminism was significant because it challenged the idea that women of the so-called "postfeminist generation" were apolitical and uninterested in furthering the gains made by the second wave of the women's movement. It

Women who won U.S. Senate races in 1992, the Year of the Woman: Patty Murray, Carol Moseley Braun, Barbara Mikulski, Dianne Feinstein, and Barbara Boxer.

© Office of U.S. Senator Dianne Feinstein

suggested that a new generation of activist, political women wanted to work together to change the world.

Under the umbrella of the Third Wave Direct Action Corporation, a nonprofit she formed with Shannon Liss, Walker and other activists organized Freedom Ride 1992, a bus tour modeled after the original freedom rides in the early 1960s. Traveling to twenty-one communities across the nation, 120 volunteers registered more than 20,000 new voters. The organization, which was renamed the Third Wave Foundation a few years later and is now known as the Third Wave Fund, refined its mission and currently sees its goal as connecting "feminist, queer, and trans organizers and donors for a stronger movement for gender, racial, and economic justice." According to its website, Third Wave is "a grassroots fund led by women of color, trans, and queer folks under the age of 35 and our allies." The ongoing work of the Third Wave Fund illustrates the willingness of young people to take action to continue the legacy of second wave feminism. It also shows a more expansive understanding of feminist activism, one that defines feminism's constituency in broader ways than second wavers would have.

Other young women made their voices heard as part of this feminist resurgence. Beginning in the early 1990s, punk rock musicians in Olympia, Washington, and Washington DC formed Riot Grrrl, a loosely connected underground movement of girls and young women in their teens and twenties. Frustrated with the sexism and misogyny of the punk music scene, Riot Grrrl musicians formed bands such as Bikini Kill, Bratmobile, Huggy Bear, and Heavens to Betsy. The name Riot Grrrl conveyed not just a revolt against society but a new way of thinking about the capacities and ideas of girls and young women; when Tobi Vail, the drummer for Bikini Kill, coined the term "grrrl," she intended it to be an aggressive, powerful growl that challenged the notion of female weakness.

In August 1991, the International Pop Underground Festival featured many of the bands that would become the main figures in the movement. In order to enact the "revolution girl style" that Riot Grrrl promoted, Bikini Kill, headed by Kathleen Hanna, challenged

Writing the Revolution

Girl Germs. Jigsaw. Chainsaw. Bamboo Girl. If you are wondering what these words have in common, they are all names of zines, self-published pamphlets that are central to third wave activism and self-expression. Although not all zines are feminist—there are zines on topics as wide-ranging as science fiction and vegetarian cooking—zines are especially identified with third wave feminism because of their connection with Riot Grrrl, which urged young women to express themselves through writing, art, and music. Many Riot Grrrls created their own zines, which, because they were self-published, empowered girls to express their critiques of society and the media without fear of censorship; by distributing their zines widely, members of Riot Grrrl began to feel connected with other like-minded girls. As one Riot Grrrl explained, "Zines are so important because so many girls feel isolated and don't have other girls to support them in their beliefs. Zines connect them to other girls who will listen and believe and care if they say they've been raped or molested or harassed." Even though Riot Grrrl peaked in the mid-1990s, zines continue to gain in popularity.

Feminist zines can have many different looks; some are handwritten, photocopied, and stapled, while others use computer graphics and professional printing. Their contents vary, too; some include sewing patterns, fashion talk, and recipes, while others have a more political focus. Many feminist zines use personal narratives in ways that are extremely different from what you would see in mainstream magazines. Indeed, the freedom to publish anything and everything inspires the creators of zines, who are not beholden to commercial publishers in any way. Although they don't make the kind of money a mainstream publisher would—many zines are distributed for free or for a nominal charge—the authors of zines don't have to worry about appealing to a market since, in many ways, they are writing to explore their own concerns.

However, some feminist zines have become so popular that they have evolved into glossy magazines, the kind you might find, if not at the supermarket checkout, then at an independent bookstore. Two such magazines are *Bust*, which was started in 1993 by Debbie Stoller and Marcelle Karp, and *Bitch: Feminist Response to Pop Culture*, created in 1996 by Lisa Jervis and Andi Zeisler.

the rules of punk performance by creating an all-female mosh pit, confronting male audience members who were being unruly and violent, and distributing song lyrics, so that listeners both could join in the performance and so that they would be able to quote the lyrics anytime they wanted in response to the sexism they encountered in their everyday lives. Like other Riot Grrrl bands, Bikini Kill wrote songs about issues of interest to girls: female friendship, sexual desire, and sexual victimization. Although they disliked punk rock's exclusion of women, Riot Grrrl embraced punk's do-it-yourself ethic, encouraging girls to learn and write music, play in bands, and create and publish zines that described their feelings.

Riot Grrrls shared their music, anger, and social critique in support groups as well as at conferences, festivals, and workshops. In July 1992, at a three-day Riot Grrrl Convention in Washington DC, bands performed, and girls exchanged zines and attended workshops on topics as diverse as eating disorders, sexual abuse, racism, and self-defense. In many ways, the discussion style embraced at this convention, at support groups, and in Riot Grrrl zines resembled the consciousness-raising of the second wave, and the similarities between radical feminism and Riot Grrrl don't stop here. While Riot Grrrls saw themselves as angrier than their feminist foremothers, the in-your-face style of Riot Grrrl was similar to the anger of radical feminists, although its confrontational posture was perhaps even more aggressive. For instance, to reclaim the word from its status as a put-down, Bikini Kill's Kathleen Hanna scrawled the word "slut" on her skin and performed songs about incest, rape, and being queer.

In spite of its ability to bring up a range of issues important to women, Riot Grrrl has been criticized for focusing mainly on the concerns of white women; the editor of *Gunk*, an early zine, expressed her disappointment with the exclusivity of Riot Grrrl: "It's like it's some secret society. . . . I constantly don't feel comfortable with this cuz I know so many girls that need to hear this shit," but aren't involved "cuz they would feel intimidated cuz they don't look punk." Other members of Riot Grrrl criticized the movement's racial homogeneity; in the zine *You Might as Well Live,*

Lauren states, "Where's the riot, white girl? And yeah some of you say we are 'out to kill white boy mentality' but have you examined your own mentality? Your white upper-middle class girl mentality? What would you say if I said that I wanted to kill that mentality too?"

As a movement, Riot Grrrl declined in the mid-1990s, at least partly in response to its appropriation and misrepresentation by the mainstream media. Instead of accurately depicting Riot Grrrl's subversive style, the media presented the movement falsely, conveying its music as a fad. The media also conflated Riot Grrrl's message with that of the pop-tart British band the Spice Girls, whose first single, "Wannabe," was released in 1996. Composed of five women, each of whom stood for a different persona of femininity—Scary Spice, Posh Spice, Baby Spice, Sporty Spice, and Ginger Spice—the Spice Girls sent a contradictory message. On the one hand, scantily dressed in miniskirts, revealing tops, and high heels, band members relied on their sexuality to sell their music. On the other hand, they sang about female friendship and claimed that their "girl power" was the decade's version of feminism. For Riot Grrrl, the message of female empowerment offered by the Spice Girls was simply too watered-down to even remotely resemble its own outraged and outrageous feminism. However, the contradictions embodied by a group such as the Spice Girls, which embraced both feminist empowerment and sexualized beauty culture, present a version of third wave feminism, which is frequently described in terms of its ability to embrace contradiction and oppositions.

If the Spice Girls are considered third wave—and many would argue they are not—it would be as part of what's known as "girlie feminism," a segment of third wave feminism that reappropriates all things considered female—baby-doll dresses, nail polish, tiny T-shirts, Hello Kitty pencil cases, not to mention the word "girl" itself, long used as a dismissive insult to infantilize adult females, such as the "girls" in the typing pool. As Jennifer Baumgardner and Amy Richards declare in *Manifesta,* "In holding tight to that which once symbolized their oppression, Girlies' motivations are along the lines of gay men in Chelsea calling each other 'queer' or black men and women using the term 'nigga.'"

In addition to reclaiming the term "girl" and embracing femininity, girlie feminists display their sexuality openly, almost as a way to counter the stereotype of feminists as asexual and frigid. Third wave feminism is cast as oppositional to the second wave at least in part because of girlie feminists' deliberate decision to deploy the trappings of femininity in a conscious, even parodic way. For many second wavers, such uses of femininity are nothing more than retrograde; they cancel out the theorizing and agitating radical feminists did, for instance, in their protest of the Miss America Pageant in 1968. For third wavers, though, incorporating "girlish" styles is a playful way to express themselves; in magazines such as *Bust*, which calls itself the magazine of the "new girl order," they find outlets for self-expression. *Bust* aims itself at girlie culture by featuring images of sexual pinup-type girls and articles such as "The Booty Myth," "I Was a Teenage Mommy," and "Blow Job Tips for Straight Women from a Gay Man." Rock critic Ann Powers explains the appeal of girlie feminism as follows: "Unlike conventional feminism, which focused on women's socially imposed weaknesses, Girl Culture assumes that women are free agents in the world, that they start out strong and that the odds are in their favor."

If we take the preceding three examples—the Third Wave Fund, Riot Grrrl, and girlie feminism—as illustrations of third wave feminism, what can we deduce about the goals, tactics, and beliefs of the third wave? Are there any commonalities among those who fall under the umbrella of the third wave as embodied by these three groups? Perhaps the most obvious common denominator has to do with age: Third wave feminism is a younger brand of feminism. In their introduction to *Third Wave Agenda: Being Feminist, Doing Feminism*, Leslie Heywood and Jennifer Drake identify third wavers as those born between 1963 and 1974; I would extend these dates to include those born in the late 1970s, the 1980s, and the 1990s. Yet, the chronological age of third wavers is less important than the fact that they grew up in a world already changed by second wave feminism. As Jennifer Baumgardner and Amy Richards write in an often-quoted passage from *Manifesta*, "[F]or anyone born after the early 1960s, the presence of feminism in our lives is taken for

Queering Femininity

Queer feminists of the third wave have theorized about femme identity—a consciously constructed queer femininity that celebrates queer desire and resists the dominant culture's values regarding conventional femininity. Many femme writers have linked their identities to a working-class background and have argued that the rejection of overt femininity espoused by some feminists has its roots in our culture's deeply held misogyny. The work of Michelle Tea, Julia Serano, and others calls to mind their femme foremothers, such as feminist lesbians Joan Nestle and Minnie Bruce Pratt, and also offers a complement to third wave feminists, writing about girlie feminism. Below is an excerpt from spoken word artist Tara Hardy's essay "Femme Dyke Slut," which appeared in the anthology *Sex and Single Girls: Straight and Queer Women on Sexuality.*

It concerns me that femmes are at best regarded as the dinosaurs of the dyke community and at worst parasites who trade on "traditional femininity" in order to pass. To begin with, femininity has never been part of my family tradition. The women in my working-class family have been workers—women with bulges due to starchy diets, feet misshapen from cheap shoes and smoker's skin even if they haven't smoked. As workers they were supposed to be asexual and not obviously gendered.

Perhaps in response to this, many in my community, including myself, choose a sexual expression that is direct, loud and unmistakable. Sadly,

granted. For our generation, feminism is like fluoride. We scarcely notice that we have it—it's simply in the water." Just as third wavers have come of age in a world shaped by feminist gains that most don't even question, they also have been influenced by forces of backlash that sometimes make them reluctant to self-identify as feminists. This belief in an equitable world alongside an exposure to backlash culture reveals another way third wavers have grown up with contradiction and oppositions, a point of view that seems "normal" to them.

The designation "third wave" is a broad one, then, and though it *this choice has often been misinterpreted. Because in a world whose watermark for being liberated is the position as far as possible from female, a loud femininity has been assumed to be extra oppressed. I believe the exact opposite is true. I think working-class women resist by stepping outside of "proper" to make a sexuality that is anything but lacking agency. In contrast to the understated, deflective femininity of the privileged, ours is a wide-mouthed, unapologetic ability to devour.*

Another means of resistance in my femininity is that it rebukes the tradition of making marginalized women—women of color, working-class and poor women—labor so the women in the middle could be fancy, uncalloused and pale. I resist constructing my femininity at the expense of another. Practically, this means I buy my clothes second-hand and not from corporations that operate sweatshops in or outside this country. I don't hire people to do shit jobs for me—one of my strongly held beliefs that has come from cleaning other people's houses is that everyone should have to scrub their own tub. I do my own laundry. I've never had a facial. I don't wear fur. I resist diets.

But I do construct my femininity, consciously. It is not by default or assigned. I choose it and sustain it. On purpose. In the dyke community there's a belief that being femme is some kind of natural expression of being female; the contradictory belief also exists that many trappings of femininity are in fact unnatural. But that crazymaking notion is not my point. My point is that I get up every day and decide how to present myself to the world, just as I witness butch, trans and FTM people laboring over how to present themselves—not because we're vain, but because how we're read is connected to safety, credibility and recognition.

may seem to include an ever-growing group of people, the same could have been said of the first wave, which lasted for almost seventy-five years. One way to make sense of the third wave's wide boundaries is by invoking the idea of "political generations." We could say that Elizabeth Cady Stanton and Susan B. Anthony were of the same political generation; they understood the women's movement in very similar ways because they joined the struggle for women's rights at almost the same time and in response to identical social limitations. Similarly, women who were radicalized after seeing news coverage of the Miss America protest and then joined a CR group could also be said to be part of a political generation; the collective identity of these women was shaped by similar experiences and interests at a particular point in history. In defining the third wave in *Catching a Wave: Reclaiming Feminism for the 21st Century*, Alison Piepmeier and I explain that "the third wave has less to do with a neat generational divide than with a cultural context: the third wave consists of those of us who have developed our sense of identity in a world shaped by technology, global capitalism, multiple models of sexuality, changing national demographics, and declining economic vitality." Even if there are differences between third wavers born in the early 1970s and those born in the early 1990s, the world we share right now sparks and renews our feminist consciousness; the third wave is wide enough to accommodate us all.

Because the world third wavers have grown up in and inhabit is so different from the one second wavers rebelled against, the third wave has a different set of interests and issues to explore and protest. In fact, third wavers have responded to issues that might not seem particularly "feminist" to some of their activist foremothers. One of the main things uniting the third wave, then, is its commitment to multiplicity, its belief that a wide range of concerns can be considered feminist. The third wave thinks about feminism more broadly than the second wave did, working to redress inequalities of all kinds, not just those based on sex. A broad-ranging set of issues interests third wavers, everything from economic injustice and global trade to welfare reform and the environment. One issue that has engaged young feminists is the movement to end sweatshop labor. After finding out that their shoes and clothing are made in crowded, unventilated, dangerous factories by young women and children who earn only pennies for their work, many students have gotten involved in the campaign to end sweatshops, joining organizations such as United Students Against Sweatshops, a group active since 1997. Similarly concerned with economic inequality were the activists who participated in the Occupy Wall Street protests that began in September 2011 in New York City and spread worldwide. Although this activism doesn't concern only women, for third wavers it is feminist nonetheless because it demands a transformation of society's power relations by calling for an end to sexist, capitalistic domination.

Unlike the second wave, which often ignored the ways women's oppressions differed depending on their race, ethnicity, economic status, and sexual orientation, the third wave is concerned with how the interlocking nature of identity helps define the causes that matter to women. For third wavers, it is not enough to think about "woman" as a broad category; to do so would be to repeat the second wave's exclusive focus on white, middle-class, heterosexual women. Instead, third wavers pick up on the work of so-called third world feminists, who worked to understand that women's lived experiences determine the oppressions they face. As Cherríe Moraga has written: "The white women's movement tried to create a new form of women's culture that on some level has denied where people come from. . . . Whether the women were Irish or German or came from working class or Jewish backgrounds, the desire to have a women's culture suddenly became devoid of race, class roots, what you ate at home, the smells in the air. Third-world feminism is talking about the vital, life-giving necessity of understanding your roots and how they influence your entire life."

For Moraga and the third wavers influenced by her work, feminism emerges out of an engagement with one's "roots." In an important essay on feminism and racism, Chela Sandoval articulated a key position that relates to Moraga's: "What U.S. third world feminists are calling for is a new subjectivity, a political revision that denies any one perspective as the only answer, but instead posits a shifting tactical and strategic subjectivity . . . no simple, easy sisterhood for U.S. third world feminists." Even if "sisterhood" is not easy, third wavers recognize the necessity of coalitions; only by listening to and learning from those who experience oppression differently can we understand the broad range of issues that need to be addressed by feminists.

The earliest third wave anthologies, Rebecca Walker's *To Be Real: Telling the Truth and Changing the Face of Feminism* and Barbara

Findlen's *Listen Up: Voices from the Next Feminist Generation,* presented the "new subjectivity" Sandoval called for, describing feminism through multiple voices, and not just through the voices of "white economically privileged heterosexual women." The authors in these collections spoke from many vantage points and perspectives and, as Findlen explained in her introduction, "call themselves, among other things, articulate, white, middle-class college kid; . . . single mother; Asian bisexual; . . . middle-class black woman; . . . member of the Muscogee (Creek) Nation; . . . a person with a visible disability; . . . lesbian daughter." As this list of voices suggests, in building on the critique of second wave feminism offered by U.S. third world feminists, third wavers insist that identity is intersectional and must be considered along all of its axes, not just one. Third wavers also have intentionally aimed to be as inclusive as possible, for instance welcoming transgendered people, who were typically excluded by lesbian groups in the second wave. "Transgender" is a broad term used to refer to people who are transsexual, gender queer (identifying with a different gender category than their bodies would predict for them), or intersex (born with ambiguous genitalia). Just as second wavers initially excluded lesbians and their concerns from feminist organizations such as NOW, feminists in the 1980s and 1990s, especially "cultural" feminists who had fairly essentialist understandings of females as naturally peaceful and nurturing, felt uncomfortable including transgendered individuals in their organizations and groups. Some feminists worried both that MTF transsexuals (male-born people who use hormones or surgery to alter their bodies and live their lives as women) were not *really* women and that they would retain the sense of male privilege they had learned from being raised as boys. But because of its suspicion of essentialist theories and its belief in the importance of difference and diversity in the composition of identity, contemporary feminism welcomes transgender feminists.

However, in spite of the third wave's desire to include multiple subjectivities, it does not, as Astrid Henry points out in "Solitary Sisterhood: Individualism Meets Collectivity in Feminism's Third Wave," wish to speak for whole groups; instead, as collections such as *To Be Real, Listen Up,* and the more recent *Colonize This! Young*

Women of Color on Today's Feminism make clear, third wavers are more interested in examining their individual identities than they are in identity politics. Indeed, as Henry and others have noted, the personal narrative is the dominant rhetorical mode of the third wave. As a result of its autobiographical tendencies, third wave feminism has been criticized, particularly by older feminists, as being too self-absorbed and not adequately political; in fact, some people see third wavers as having little interest in a feminist "movement" as such.

Also as a result of its insistence on multiple, personal voices, critics—as well as academics—have found it difficult to pin down the central beliefs of the third wave. Third wavers often define their feminism in terms of its opposition to the feminism that preceded it; many see themselves and their identities as in conflict with their second wave feminist foremothers. Although essays in both *Listen Up* and *To Be Real* articulate the idea of generational conflict, Rebecca Walker's introduction to *To Be Real* encapsulates this stance, stating: "For many of us it seems that to be a feminist in the way that we have seen or understood feminism is to conform to an identity and way of living that doesn't allow for individuality, complexity, or less than perfect personal histories. We fear that the identity will dictate and regulate our lives, instantaneously pitting us against someone, forcing us to choose inflexible and unchanging sides, female against male, black against white, oppressed against oppressor, good against bad."

Walker's depiction of the second wave, like many that would follow it, evokes an image of a repressive, puritanical, even dogmatic mother who would school her unruly daughter into submission to her political beliefs. In some ways, this image resembles the stereotypical anti-sex feminist who taught women's studies classes at colleges in the 1980s and early 1990s. Although many third wavers feel distant from what they see as the stern orthodoxy of the second wave, the rehearsal of this collective disavowal of the second wave often relies more on impressionistic understandings of earlier feminisms than on solid engagement with the history of feminist movements.

Like second wave feminists, third wavers share the desire to

"Power" Feminism

Although the media have devoted much attention to stories about post-feminism, announcing with surprising regularity the "death" of feminism, third wave feminism is not synonymous with postfeminism. In fact, even if they see themselves as very different from their feminist foremothers, young feminists recognize a continuing need for activism to end the inequalities faced by people disadvantaged by sex, color, class, sexual orientation, or disability. However, in the early 1990s, when third wave feminism was first discussed in the media, self-proclaimed feminist authors promoted their own writing by rehashing the idea that feminism was outmoded and that feminists were whiny victims. As a result, the media conflated the ideas of these "feminist dissenters" with third wave feminism itself.

Yet, if we look at the work of people such as Katie Roiphe, Rene Denfeld, and even Naomi Wolf, we can see attitudes out of sync with feminism's focus on collective action. In *The Morning After: Sex, Fear, and Feminism*, Katie Roiphe, herself the daughter of a second wave feminist, complains about the way feminist theory and activism in the violence against women movement have cast women as victims. In particular, Roiphe questions the movement to end violence on college campuses; in her view, work to

end sexism and sexist oppression, and to do that, they work within organizations formed by their feminist predecessors, organizations such as the National Organization for Women, Planned Parenthood, and the National Women's Political Caucus. They also perform activist work in organizations they have created themselves. For instance, the National Latina Institute for Reproductive Health (NLIRH), founded in 1994, seeks health, dignity, and justice for the millions of Latinas living in the United States. Focusing on three aspects of reproductive justice—access to abortion, sexual and reproductive health equity, and the rights of immigrant women—NLIRH works to remake society so that Latinas "have the economic means, social capital, and political power to make and exercise decisions about their own health, family, and future." Begun in 2007, the National Domestic end date rape has led to a "culture of caution" antithetical to the sexual freedom supposedly promoted by second wavers. Rene Denfeld's *The New Victorians: A Young Woman's Challenge to the Old Feminist Order* echoes Roiphe's critique of the repressiveness and rigidity of the second wave. Unlike Roiphe, however, Denfeld moves beyond a critique, offering what she refers to as "equality feminism" as the solution to the problems with contemporary feminism. By endorsing a feminism engaged with promoting equal rights and opportunities, Denfeld hoped to inject feminism with new energy. So, too, did Naomi Wolf, who, in *Fire with Fire: The New Female Power and How It Will Change the 21st Century*, argues for a "power feminism" that would replace the "victim feminism" bequeathed by the second wave. According to Wolf, women need to take charge of their own lives, and that means seizing economic, political, and sexual power.

There are a number of problems with these books. First, they offer a fairly reductive depiction of second wave feminism, focusing only on sexual rigidity and puritanical attitudes connected with victimhood. Second, the solutions offered by Denfeld and Wolf rely on the individual, ultimately promoting individualism as a way to remedy the faults of feminism. Power feminism serves only to empty feminism of the collective action that motivated it in the first and second waves.

Workers Alliance (NDWA) advocates for those who work as nannies, housekeepers, and caregivers for the elderly; because this workforce is excluded from almost all labor laws, the NDWA fights for improved working conditions, better labor protections, and the recognition of an important, but often overlooked, workforce. Another group trying to help a marginalized population is the Sylvia Rivera Law Project (SRLP), which started in 2002; the group supports transgender, intersex, and gender non-conforming people. Because of its understanding of the ways that gender inequality is connected to racial, ethnic, and economic inequality, the SLRP "works to guarantee that all people are free to self-determine their gender identity and expression, regardless of income or race, and without facing harassment, discrimination, or violence." These organizations are working in a variety of ways—

changing laws, counseling clients, and training individuals through leadership development programs.

Some third wave organizations aim their activism at girls and teens; for instance, the Rock 'n' Roll Camp for Girls, which began in 2001 in Portland, Oregon, gives girls a chance to create and perform music, thereby increasing their confidence, self-esteem, and leadership skills. Inspired by the Portland camp, women in other cities, including Atlanta, Boston, Chicago, and Las Vegas, have formed their own branches of girls rock camps. Another nonprofit designed to involve girls in a male-dominated field, Girls Who Code, which began in 2012, aims to teach girls computing skills so they can work in technology and engineering fields after college. Starting with only one program in New York City, by 2014 the organization created over 160 clubs in schools, libraries, and community centers across the country. It hopes to provide education in computer science to one million young women by 2020. Another organization dedicated to young women is Girls Educational and Mentoring Service (GEMS), which works to help girls and young women to leave the commercial sex industry. Although GEMS seeks an end to the commercial sexual exploitation and trafficking of girls, it is less an anti-trafficking organization and more of an advocacy group that focuses on giving survivors of "the life" a chance to develop their potential, providing them with financial, educational, psychological, and emotional support as they work to rebuild their lives, find housing, get an education, and secure a job.

The activism that has caught the public's attention recently has to do with ending rape culture. This activism is wide-ranging and illustrates a variety of modes of organizing, some reminiscent of the second wave and some reliant on newer methods. This organizing began as a response to a number of things, including the Office for Civil Rights' "Dear Colleague Letter," which mandated that colleges and universities enforce Title IX regulations more stringently, the Office's investigation of Yale University for creating a hostile environment for students, and students' realization that they could file Title IX complaints against their own institutions for their schools' response to their sexual assaults. For instance, the students Annie Clark and Andrea Pino filed a complaint in 2013 against the University of North Carolina for its handling of campus sexual assaults. Because of what they learned about the difficulty of navigating the system, the two women started the organization End Rape on Campus (EROC) to help provide resources not just to survivors of sexual violence but to parents, alumni, and faculty. The goal of EROC is to help survivors who wish to file complaints with the Office for Civil Rights. A similar organization is Know Your IX; founded in 2013 by Dana Bolger and Alexandra Brodsky, it focuses on ending campus sexual violence. According to its website, Know Your IX works "to educate our fellow students about their rights and empower them to take action for safety and equality on campus." The documentary *The Hunting Ground* (2015), which discusses the epidemic of rape on college campuses and focuses on Clark and Pino's activism in particular, shows how the two women's work connects to the work done by the feminists who preceded them: even though the Internet, social media, and cell phones allow the activists to collaborate easily with the survivors they are seeking to help, much of Clark and Pino's activism is slow-going since it involves traveling the country, meeting with survivors, teaching them how to file complaints, and finding out how to intervene in a variety of sluggish bureaucracies. The triumphs they feel as a result of their grassroots organizing are very real, but they do not come about quickly, in spite of the availability of technology.

In some cases, contemporary activism varies greatly from that done by second wavers, sometimes because of technology and other times because of a very different set of political commitments. For example, Hollaback!, a nonprofit that began in 2005, is a group interested in protesting street harassment and in making public spaces safer and more equitable. The organization relies heavily on people's ability to capture instances of street harassment on their smart phones and then share these films or pictures through social media. Another third wave activist group, which uses theatrical public protests more akin to the

© Julie Freburg, 2002

Lickity Split Radical Cheerleaders, Chicago. From left to right: Rasheedah Shahid (Coco Muff), Abby Katz (Queefer Sutherland), Amy Miller (Pussy Elliott), and Susan Ashman (cunt a liscious).

zap actions of second wavers, has a different kind of feminist politics than earlier second wave groups. The Radical Cheerleaders began with two activist sisters in Florida, but the group has spread across the globe, with squads all over the United States and as far overseas as Poland. Although the group is not as ubiquitous as it was in the 2000s, its activism offers a clear illustration of third wave politics. As the website of the New York branch states, "Radical cheerleading is protest with pom poms, dissent with middle fingers extended. [T]ired of the same left, right, left, radical cheerleaders reinvigorate the idea of political protest by making it fun to participate in dissent." Members of squads meet to rehearse cheers and then perform them at political protests, such as the March for Women's Lives held in Washington DC in April 2004. Some of the group's cheers, which are reproduced on its website, reveal a politics similar to that of the radical feminists who protested the Miss America Pageant in 1968. For instance, in "Riot, Don't Diet," the Cheerleaders say:

hey girl (clap clap clap)
get yer face out of that magazine
you are more than a beauty machine
you've got anger soul and more
take to the street and let it roar
RIOT DON'T DIET
GET UP GET OUT AND TRY IT
RIOT DON'T DIET
GET UP GET OUT AND TRY IT

The cheer goes on to urge its listeners to send *Cosmopolitan* "some hate mail" and to "liberate the beauty queen / from the shackles of the fashion scene." In spite of its punchy enthusiasm, this cheer is reminiscent of the kind of critique of beauty culture offered by Robin Morgan in her analysis of Miss America.

Yet, another cheer, "Queerleaders," reveals a more third wave sensibility:

We're sexy we're cute
we're feminist to boot
we're angry, we're tough
and we have had enough
we're butchy, we're femme
we're transgender girls and men
we spank it, we roar
we support our local whore
we're here, we're queer
we slept with britney spears
hate us cuz we're sex positive?
well, we don't like you neither
we're queerleaders
we are queerleaders

Here, the Radical Cheerleaders explode the stereotypical image of the feminist, proclaiming that they are "sexy" and "cute." Second wavers would never have felt comfortable making such a pronouncement, since it would seem to challenge their own critique of beauty culture. While the cheer acknowledges feminist anger and toughness, traits of the second wave, to be sure, its embrace of multiple sexual orientations and identities—lesbian, queer, transgender—would have been difficult to accomplish during the second wave, which was dominated by fear of a "lavender menace" as well as by gay-straight splits and lesbian separatism. The cheer's promotion of a pro-sex message—through "support" of prostitutes and its outright proclamation of its sex-positive stance—is another way of allying itself with the third wave. Finally, the playfulness of the chant, along with its engagement with pop culture—its reference to Britney Spears, for instance—reveals the third wave's insistence on pleasure and lightheartedness.

In extending the legacy of the second wave with a more playful spirit, the third wave certainly runs the risk of being criticized as being lightweight and frivolous. Yet, it seems unfazed by this criticism, unwilling to let its different approach to feminist activism mean that its voice will not be heard or taken seriously. In addition to being radicalized in women's studies classes on college campuses, third wavers continue to publish articles and books, including texts such as *Female Chauvinist Pigs: Women and the Rise of Raunch Culture, Perfect Girls, Starving Daughters: How the Quest for Perfection Is Harming Young Women,* and *Bad Feminist.* They are also visible online, on blogs such as Feministing, Jezebel, and Feministe, and on video web series such as Feminist Frequency, which examines the representations of women in popular culture. Many operate within pop culture itself, using comedy as a way to critique society's expectations of women. Almost ten years ago, Sarah Haskins's segment "Target Women" on the TV show *infoMania* ridiculed everything from women's supposed obsession with yogurt to the bogus science used in skin care commercials. More recently, sketch comedy shows such as *Portlandia* and *Inside Amy Schumer* grapple with feminist politics, as do the series *Broad City* and *Girls,* which feature young women who are trying to figure out how to operate as adults in New York City. Although these examples vary widely, they illustrate the fact that third wave feminism is alive, vibrant, and ready to expose, discuss, and, even, redress inequality in all its guises.

Chapter 5

Knowing Our History, Changing Our Future

IN REFLECTING ON NEARLY 170 YEARS of feminist movement in the United States, it's hard not to feel a surge of pride; in this time, women have accomplished many things, gaining the right to vote, educational and work opportunities, and access to reproductive rights, to name only the most obvious achievements of feminist activists. As significant as these gains is the shift that has occurred in the dominant understanding of women's roles; whereas historically women have been identified with their domestic and nurturing duties, because of feminism, women have become free to take on public, intellectual, and even physical roles—as carpenters, electricians, and athletes, as businesswomen, doctors, and police officers, as legislators, judges, and labor leaders. Because of the work women can now do, the world we inhabit in the 21st century could hardly be more different from the one women encountered during the first and second waves of the women's movement.

But what about feminism today? In spite of the expanded roles and opportunities women have because of earlier waves of feminism, many women are reluctant to identify with feminism, which they view as an "f-word," something dangerous and profane, an explosive term angry, unfeminine women use to identify themselves. It doesn't help, either, that the mainstream media misrepresent feminists, or that misinformed people such as Christian Coalition founder Pat Robertson make statements such as the following: "The feminist agenda is not about equal rights for women. It is about a socialist, anti-family political movement that encourages women to leave their husbands, kill their children, practice witchcraft, destroy capitalism, and become lesbians." Given such erroneous characterizations of feminism, it's hardly surprising that young women wish to distance themselves from it. Even so, these women often say, "I'm not a feminist, but . . . " and then go on to state their support for feminist goals: that women should have the right to live in a world without violence or sexual harassment, that husbands should share childcare responsibilities, and that women should have access to reproductive choice. As Lisa Maria Hogeland has stated in "Fear of Feminism: Why Young Women Get the Willies," college women are afraid of feminism because it represents a daunting, challenging political commitment. It is far easier, she claims, to rest in gender consciousness, the awareness and celebration of women's difference from men, than it is to take the leap toward feminist consciousness, which would require sustained cultural analysis and action.

Among self-identified feminists, other problems exist, including a debate about the merits of the wave metaphor as a way of understanding and classifying feminism. In a speech delivered at the annual conference of the National Women's Studies Association in 2004 and later published in *Ms.* magazine as "The End of Feminism's Third Wave," Lisa Jervis, the cofounder of the magazine *Bitch: Feminist Response to Pop Culture,* stated: "We've reached the end of the wave terminology's usefulness. What was at first a handy-dandy way to refer to feminism's history and its present and future potential with a single metaphor has become shorthand that invites intellectual laziness, an escape hatch from the hard work of distinguishing between core beliefs and a cultural moment." Jervis rejects an easy and uncomplicated acceptance of "third wave" as a feminist classification, mainly because an uncritical use of the term promotes division among second and third wavers, who are actually working to accomplish very similar goals.

Whereas Jervis questions the need for categorization by feminist waves, some younger feminists claim allegiance to the fourth wave. When Jennifer Baumgardner interviewed the twenty-something activist Shelby Knox in 2010, Knox expressed her belief in a fourth wave, a wave that has to do with the discovery of feminist values through blogging and social media. Knox explains that technology allows young feminists to think through the issues that matter to them and figure out their ideological stances. In addition, she asserts that blogs in particular "have equalized feminism, because you don't have to have the money to be in a women's studies class or be able-bodied enough to attend a consciousness-raising group every week or to stand on a picket line." In an essay titled "Is There a Fourth Wave? Does It Matter?," Baumgardner writes that, through blogs and tweets on topics as varied as trans issues, fashion, and reproductive rights, the fourth wave has put into practice the ideas theorized by third wave feminists.

Perhaps because of my involvement in theorizing the third wave and because of my interest in history, I have difficulty with an uncomplicated acceptance of the fourth wave. I am ready neither to declare an "end" to the third wave nor to claim the existence of a fourth wave, though I do acknowledge that younger women can engage with both feminist and antifeminist ideas extremely easily as a result of the internet, technology, and social media. I am more interested in deemphasizing the divisions between feminist generations than I am in demanding the recognition of a new wave.

Instead of focusing on the distinctions between second and third wavers or claiming the existence of a fourth wave of feminism, approaching feminism as a collective project aimed at eradicating sexism and domination seems the most practical way to continue feminist work. Quibbling about which wave we are currently in or whether I think of myself as a second, third, or fourth waver hardly seems like a good use of my limited time; instead, I'd like to see sustained feminist activism performed by young, middle-aged, and old women separately or, better yet, together. A recent project that deemphasizes the wave metaphor and even the necessity of identifying as a feminist is the Who Needs Feminism? campaign. Begun in 2012 by students in a class on Women in the Public Sphere at Duke University, Who Needs Feminism? is essentially a public relations campaign for feminism. As a way to dismantle stigmas associated with feminism and to show

The V-Word

One of the best examples of an activist project that cannot be pigeonholed into one wave or another is *The Vagina Monologues*. A series of monologues written and initially performed by Eve Ensler in 1996, the play both celebrates women's bodies and sexualities and protests the violence committed against them. Ensler wrote *The Vagina Monologues* after interviewing more than two hundred women about sex, relationships, and violence against women; the play she created in response to these interviews centers around women's sexuality, a topic that is rarely covered openly and honestly in the mass media. The play's title alone has been controversial; at some schools where the play is produced, merely advertising the play has led to debate and even censorship, as some people are uncomfortable with the "v-word." In spite of this squeamishness, the play has developed a huge following: It has been translated into more than twenty languages and has been staged throughout the world.

The play's monologues take as their subject matter everything connected with the vagina: love and relationships; sex, orgasm, and masturbation; rape and mutilation; and menstruation and birth. One of the monologues, "The Little Coochie Snorcher That Could," has been criticized for its depiction of what could be seen as statutory rape. In this sketch, a woman remembers sexual traumas from her past as well as a positive sexual experience she had with an older woman when

how feminism is still necessary, the students devised a way to showcase individual people's explanations of why they need feminism. Instead of defining feminism in an explicit way or even asking individuals to claim that they are feminists, the campaign encouraged people to articulate the utility of feminism, what feminism can do. After writing why they needed feminism on a sheet of paper on a white board, people were photographed holding their statements. These pictures were then shared electronically as well as turned into posters which were displayed around campus. An op-ed the students wrote explaining the campaign was published in the campus newspaper at the same time as the posters were placed around campus. The campaign at Duke went viral, gained she was a teenager. When the monologue was first performed, the woman was thirteen at the time of the latter sexual experience; Ensler raised her age to sixteen in later productions. Ensler's play has received other criticisms as well; some people object to what they view as an anti-male and anti-heterosexual tone in the play. Some feminists argue that, while its celebration of female sexuality is positive, the play reduces women to their biology. Instead of depicting the complexity of women's experience—women have brains as well as vaginas, after all—the play can be seen to essentialize women's identities. For many women, however, *The Vagina Monologues* is a positive, empowering play, and it helps to expose the general public to affirmative depictions of female sexuality as well as to the damaging effects of violence against women and girls.

Although Ensler performed all of the monologues herself at first, as the play gained critical attention, it developed into a three-woman show, starring actresses such as Susan Sarandon, Glenn Close, and Whoopi Goldberg. The play is now performed annually on college campuses nationwide, where it is the centerpiece of V-Day, a nonprofit movement established by Ensler and other activists to end violence against women. As part of its college initiative, V-Day gives universities and colleges permission to stage the play; in return, these institutions donate proceeds from the performance to community organizations dedicated to ending violence against women and girls. As a result of this initiative, more than $14 million has been raised globally.

much national attention, and sparked similar activism at other colleges and universities across the country and around the world. In 2013, as part of a class I teach on contemporary women's movements, my students conducted a Who Needs Feminism? campaign at Vanderbilt University.

Concentrating on divisions between feminist generations ignores the continuities between present-day activists and their feminist foremothers. Much of the work that is ongoing among feminist activists today represents a continuation of the work begun by women in the past. For instance, violence against women has concerned activists since at least the nineteenth century, when women involved in the temperance movement wanted to outlaw alcohol because, among other reasons, inebriated men often committed violent acts against their wives and families. In 1978, late in the second wave, members of San Francisco's Women Against Violence in Pornography and Media organized a march through the city's red-light district, and thousands of people demonstrated against the sexism of pornography that eroticizes and normalizes violence against women. They called their march Take Back the Night. As the march gained publicity, other organizations, mainly women's centers and feminist groups at colleges and universities, borrowed the idea; now many of these groups include Take Back the Night as part of their yearly calendars. Instead of being a protest against porn, however, the event publicizes the problems of acquaintance rape and sexual assault, which affect women on campus in very direct ways. Although individual institutions approach Take Back the Night differently, the event typically includes a speak-out, at which victims of violence tell their stories—a tactic first used by second wave feminists—as well as a candlelit march in which participants both protest the lack of safety women experience in going about their daily lives and challenge the community to come together to ensure that violence against women stops.

Younger feminists have devised other ways to challenge sexual assault and rape culture. Starting in 2011, they have participated in SlutWalks, protests that center on the ways that victims are blamed for the violence that has been done to them. The first SlutWalk occurred in Toronto after a police officer stated that, in order to prevent instances of sexual victimization, "women should avoid dressing like sluts." Although the police officer later apologized for his "slut-shaming" remarks, Heather Jarvis and Sonya Barrett, the co-founders of SlutWalk Toronto, felt that they needed to do something to protest a society that blames women for being sexually assaulted. The two women planned a march in April 2011, expecting that about 200 people would come; instead, 3000 people protested, some wearing high heels and short skirts, others dressed in sneakers and T-shirts. Activists held signs that read "Don't Tell Us How to Dress; Tell Him Not to Rape" and "My Clothes Are Not My Consent." The protest gained much media attention and sparked similar public actions in 200 countries. SlutWalks continue, though they have received their share of criticism for their allegedly unreflective use of the male-defined word "slut" to describe participants, their uncritical equation of sexuality and liberation, and for the potential exclusion of black women, for whom being called a slut has a different historical meaning. In spite of these critiques, SlutWalks illustrate how younger activists have developed ways to protest victim blaming and violence against women that differ from those created by their feminist precursors.

Just as violence against women is an issue feminist activists have addressed throughout the history of American feminism, women since the nineteenth century have challenged a beauty culture that imposes impossible ideals on females of all ages. During the first wave, proponents of dress reform advocated looser clothing, arguing that the multiple layers worn by women were excessive and impeded natural movement. Women in the twentieth century continued to challenge beauty ideals that kept women focused on how they looked rather than on what they did. Second wave feminists fought beauty standards that asked them to use makeup, curlers, and false eyelashes in order to appear beautiful and to wear skirts, girdles, panty hose, and high heels so they would seem "feminine." Second wavers opposed advertisements that objectified women as well; in her memoir of the women's movement, Susan Brownmiller discusses how the group Media Women posted stickers reading THIS AD INSULTS WOMEN on offensive ads in the New York City subways. This was certainly not the only group to perform such an action. Naomi Wolf's critique of repressive beauty standards in her 1991 bestseller, *The Beauty Myth,* extended second wavers' criticisms from twenty years before. Wolf's discussion of beauty, pornography, and eating disorders reveals the pernicious nature of the more recent beauty ideal. According to Wolf, unlike their foremothers who wore girdles to mold their bodies, girls and young women today wear girdles "made of their own flesh." Wolf argues that the contemporary world is so hostile to women's advancement that women's psyches suffer as much damage as their bodies because of the unrealistic ideals they are asked to uphold. Much writing of the third wave has examined the unhealthy images that imprison young women today; indeed, the activist and author Amy Richards has written, "Body image . . . may be the pivotal third wave issue—the common struggle that mobilizes the current feminist generation."

While white women have written powerfully on the way the dominant culture's ideals have helped to shape, even corrupt, their sense of beauty, black women also have expressed their dissatisfaction with the way mainstream beauty ideals exclude women of color or else suggest that their beauty is inferior to the white standard. Sirena J. Riley's "The Black Beauty Myth," published in *Colonize This!*, reminds us that problems with body image affect all women, that these problems are part of the "common struggle" Richards discusses. In her essay, Riley states, "Just because women of color aren't expressing their body dissatisfaction in the same way as heterosexual, middle-class white women, it doesn't mean that everything is hunky-dory and we should just move on." Speaking out about her relationship with her body helps to ensure that body image isn't perceived as an issue that affects only white women. Similarly, Kiri Davis's short documentary film *A Girl Like Me* represents an effort to educate the public about the attitudes about beauty held by young black women. In the film, a number of black women speak about their dissatisfaction with their appearances; their kinky hair and dark skin do not meet the standards created by the dominant white culture, which prizes blondness, whiteness, and thinness. A number of women in the film describe the bleaching creams used by dark women to lighten their skin; one woman talks about a mother who put bleaching cream on her daughters starting when they were very young. During the black nationalist movement of the 1960s, activists coined the slogan "Black is beautiful"; Davis's film is a contemporary challenge to lingering racism and sexism in a culture that still perpetuates the idea that black is not beautiful.

Other activist work continues to be done to educate the public about beauty ideals that harm women and girls. Created in 1991 by Sut

Jhally, a professor of communication at the University of Massachusetts, the Media Education Foundation researches contemporary media issues and produces and distributes educational resources, mainly documentary films. Some of the most powerful documentaries I show in my introductory women's and gender studies courses have been created through the Media Education Foundation: Jhally's analysis of advertising images in *The Codes of Gender,* Jackson Katz's discussion of masculinity and violence in *Tough Guise 2,* and Jessica Valenti's argument about the retrograde use of young women's sexuality in *The Purity Myth.* While the Media Education Foundation may be aimed more at educators and their students than at the general public, *Miss Representation,* a documentary that premiered at the Sundance Film Festival in 2011, has had a wider release, particularly since it was acquired by the Oprah Winfrey Network. *Miss Representation* examines the ways that contemporary media shortchanges girls and women by portraying them as having value only because of their appearance, and not because of their intellect, power, or leadership abilities. Another more mainstream critique of beauty ideals is the website About-face.org, which "equips women and girls with tools to understand and resist harmful media messages that affect self-esteem and body image." Focusing particularly on advertising images, About-face collects ads that depict women in negative ways and displays them in its "Gallery of Offenders." Although such an action might seem to be giving further publicity to retrograde images, the website also assembles ads that present women positively and places these in a "Gallery of Winners." About-face also offers resources for activism, including books, web links, and the addresses of companies. It encourages people to respond to the ads that offend them by thinking critically, spending carefully, and using their voices to protest. In many ways a descendant of the second wave feminists who identified sexist ads in the 1960s and '70s, About-face uses its website, along with a blog it has set up, to spread its message that media stereotypes can be resisted.

Feminists today are extending the work of their predecessors in other ways as well, particularly through their critiques of important social institutions. Just as second wave feminists fought for access for all women to contraception and abortion, for women's inclusion in research studies, and for their autonomy over their medical decisions, contemporary activists continue to work to make healthcare more accessible to women, especially poor women, women of color, and transgender women. Activists are fighting for a universal healthcare system, one that does not discriminate against people based on their sex, race, ethnicity, class, sexual orientation, or disability. Because our current healthcare system is so dependent not just on private insurance and health management organizations but also on pharmaceutical companies, some feminists have critiqued the marketing of drugs that heal everything from menopause to depression.

Perhaps the most pressing issue contemporary feminism is engaging with—and one that I want to examine in some depth—has to do with

Can Men Be Feminists?

I ask my students this question after we read "Real Men Join the Movement," an article that the sociologist Michael Kimmel published in *Ms.* magazine in the late 1990s. The author of countless books and articles on men, masculinity, and sexuality, Kimmel refers to himself and other men who believe in feminist goals as "profeminist men," and not as "feminist men" or "male feminists." As Kimmel explains, "[F]eminism involves an empirical observation—that women are not equal—and the moral position that declares they should be." According to Kimmel, men can certainly support feminist ideals and play an "auxiliary" role in feminist movements, following women's lead, but they cannot call themselves feminists because feminism "involves the felt experience of . . . inequality. And this men do not have, because men are privileged by sexism. . . . [M]en are not oppressed *as men.* Since only women have that felt experience of oppression about gender, it seems sensible to make a distinction in how we identify ourselves."

Kimmel's logic makes a lot of sense; perhaps men should not say they are feminists because they can never know what it's like to be oppressed because of their sex. Yet, upon further reflection, there are problems with disallowing men from calling themselves feminist. First of all, because the goal of feminism is equality, it is only fair to offer both men and women finding a balance between work and parenthood. In the introduction to *The F-Word: Feminism in Jeopardy: Women, Politics, and the Future*, Kristin Rowe-Finkbeiner writes, "Motherhood, particularly the social and economic burden facing women with children, is perhaps the principal feminist issue for today's young women, with surveys showing that many women in college are already concerned about balancing work and motherhood in the future." Later in the book, Rowe-Finkbeiner elaborates on this idea, stating that "the new feminist issues" are "paid family leave; affordable, safe, and educational child care; equal educational opportunities; the maternal wage gap; managing the varied roles of women and parents; and counting the unpaid work of parents in places like the U.S. Census." Rowe-Finkbeiner isn't the only person discussing the intersection of work and family, but her nomination of

equal access to feminism. Just as important, the reasoning that we must "feel" inequality to identify with feminism is flawed. What if you are a female who has experienced much privilege in her life? Do you not qualify as a feminist unless you have experienced sexism directly? Insisting that feminism involves a "felt experience" thus limits the ranks of potential feminists. It also risks asking people to compare their oppressions—as in, "You may have 'felt' this one form of oppression, but I've felt these five forms. I think I'm more qualified to be a feminist than you are." Such comparison is dangerous since it would seem to establish a hierarchical ranking of those who qualify as feminists. Feminism would be a pretty exclusive social movement if only those people whose oppression met some criteria were "qualified" to call themselves feminists.

Although this topic is open to debate, I say, if your boyfriend, husband, brother, father—or any male person you know, for that matter—is committed to ending sexism and domination, he should feel free to call himself a feminist. The gains for feminism are great: more people to extend feminism's goals. And the gains for individual men are significant as well: Thanks to feminism, men can learn to embrace traits often devalued as "feminine," traits such as cooperation, nurturance, communication, and emotional self-expression, qualities that will enable them more fully to embrace their humanity.

the issue as central to young women indicates that it's not just policy makers and academics who care about the issue of work-family balance but also people who are about to enter into the work world and begin families of their own. They want to be able to thrive in both arenas of their lives, and the current system makes this pretty hard to do.

Although balancing work and family is a crucial issue for today's feminists, it is not new: It has its roots in first and second wavers' fight for access to equal employment opportunities. Unfortunately, earlier activists couldn't fully anticipate the challenges women would face once they began to work outside the home in greater and greater numbers— or the economic and cultural changes that would accompany this shift. As the activism of second wavers succeeded and more and more women sought careers in addition to marriage and family, a new ideal emerged: the Superwoman. This icon of the 1980s wore "power" suits, often with oversize shoulder pads that made her look more "masculine," and carried both a briefcase and a baby as she rushed out the door. While this caricature caught the public's attention, so did the new realities of combining work with family. In a famous formulation, sociologist Arlie Hochschild talked about the "second shift" of housework and childcare performed by women who work outside the home; unlike men, women are more responsible for the brunt of household chores and suffer from exhaustion and anger as a result. Instead of thinking about ways of alleviating women's burdens at home, most of the talk about women and careers in the 1980s had to do with the fact that women weren't achieving as much as they expected to. Although opinions differ on who coined the term "glass ceiling," it first appeared in print in 1984 in a profile of Gay Bryant, then the editor of *Working Woman* magazine, and in Bryant's book *The Working Woman Report: Succeeding in Business in the 80s*. In the latter, Bryant writes:

> *Throughout the corporate world—faster in some industries, slower in others—the door to real power for women has opened. But it is just ajar. Women may already be in middle management, but the steps from there up to the senior*

hierarchy are likely to be slow and painstakingly small. Partly because corporations are structured as pyramids, with many middle managers trying to move up into the few available spots, and partly because of continuing, though more subtle, discrimination, a lot of women are hitting a "glass ceiling" and finding they can rise no further.

Even if people did not read Bryant's book, they may have heard of the glass ceiling when an article of that name was published in *The Wall Street Journal* in 1986. Thirty years later, women still feel the effects of the glass ceiling: for an example, we need to look no farther than the settlement of a case against Outback Steakhouse. In 2009, Outback agreed to pay $19 million to settle a class lawsuit brought by thousands of women who worked at the restaurant chain. According to the suit, Outback discriminated against female employees, who could not reach top management positions because they were excluded from the kitchen management jobs that would give them the experience they needed to be eligible for promotion. Cases like these aren't rare, unfortunately; in 2015, a case was filed against Twitter by women who claim that the company does not promote female engineers into leadership positions.

Although these cases show that women can take legal action in response to discrimination, such a route is costly. More often, women alter their own work patterns instead of trying to change corporate policies. In 1989, Felice Schwartz, the founder of Catalyst, a nonprofit organization that focuses on women and business, published an article in the *Harvard Business Review* in which she argued that many women need greater flexibility in their work lives to accommodate the demands of their families. Her proposal, which suggested lighter workloads and more manageable schedules—what was referred to by others as a "Mommy Track"—was extremely controversial among feminists. While some feminists responded positively, arguing that Schwartz's ideas offered a creative approach to combining work and motherhood, others worried that the Mommy Track would create conditions that would naturalize women's lack of promotions and lower pay. Just as important, some feminists thought that, instead of challenging women's social roles, Schwartz assumed that women were, or should be, the primary caregivers in their families. Instead of asking men to shoulder more of the burdens of home life, Schwartz's proposal reinforced the stereotype that these were women's responsibility.

While the issue of mothers and the workplace remained important during the 1990s, it gained much public attention in the new millennium, particularly in response to "The Opt-Out Revolution," a story written by Lisa Belkin and published in the *New York Times Magazine* in October 2003. Belkin's article examined how a group of privileged women whose elite educations were made possible by feminism decided to leave the workforce after the birth of their children. These women seemed happy with this choice, and Belkin suggested that their decision was somehow "revolutionary." While statistics published by the U.S. Census Bureau reveal that the number of mothers of infants who are returning to work is definitely on the decline—59 percent of these mothers returned to work in 1998, 55 percent in 2000, and 54.6 percent in 2002—it's important to realize that many of these mothers do go back to work after their children reach the age of one. Although the women profiled by Belkin may be at the vanguard of a national trend of at least short-term stay-at-home motherhood, the values they promote—quality time spent with children and a redefinition of what constitutes success—appealing as they may be, hardly apply to most women, who, though they might love to quit work and be with their children, cannot afford such a "choice."

One of the most critical responses to Belkin's article came from Linda Hirshman, who published the essay "Homeward Bound" in the *American Prospect* in 2005 and the short book *Get to Work: A Manifesto for Women of the World* in 2006. In both pieces, Hirshman urged those who would be inclined to opt out to return to their jobs instead. Hirshman argues that young women need to take their educations seriously, study something that will land them high-paying jobs, and not quit their jobs when a child comes along. Dismayed by the percentage of women with advanced degrees in law and business who have abandoned work to start families, Hirshman wants to see more women further their careers and gain economic power. To that end, she lays out some practical rules, including marrying someone with an undemanding job and having only one child. The idea seems to be that a husband who is less committed to his work, along with a smaller family and a household managed by both parents, will allow a woman to devote most of her energies to career building.

Sheryl Sandberg, the Chief Operating Officer of Facebook, continued this discussion of work–life balance in a TED talk she gave in 2010, a commencement address she delivered at Barnard College in 2011, and, most famously, in her bestselling book *Lean In: Women, Work and the Will to Lead* (2013). Although her tone is far less castigating than Hirshman's, Sandberg similarly urges women to maintain a high level of commitment to work, warning them not to "leave before you leave"; that is, women should not start thinking about ways to scale back their work lives to allow for more flexibility even before they have children. Instead, they should "lean in" to their work so they can advance in their careers as much as possible. In short, they should think big about their work and "aspire to leadership," something their socialization as females has not encouraged them to do. Sandberg also advises that women be prudent about selecting their partner, stating that "who you marry is the single most important career decision you make." Unlike Hirshman, who suggests that women marry someone whose career can take a backseat to theirs, Sandberg encourages women to marry someone whose career is important, but who will support their career by being an equal partner in every way, particularly by splitting household responsibilities equally.

The impact of Sandberg's "feminist manifesto" has been enormous. The book has sold more than two million copies worldwide and spawned more than 22,700 "Lean In" circles in 110 countries. In these circles, or small groups, women meet on a regular basis to discuss their professional goals and to keep each other committed to achieving them. In spite of its success, *Lean In* has received criticism for focusing on the situation of a specific group of women—mainly well-educated, privileged professionals. Its advice ignores the experience of poorer women, those who do not have the kind of "compelling, challenging, and rewarding job" that makes leaving a child with a caregiver financially feasible. Others have criticized Sandberg for turning the issue of work–life balance into an individual problem that can be solved when women grow more ambitious and cast off a gender socialization that taught them to be passive. In addition, Sandberg's belief that having more women leaders will yield better policies for women in the workplace neglects the fact that not all women leaders have all women's interests at heart. Sandberg's position ignores the structural inequalities that cannot be dismantled by individual self-motivation.

Anne-Marie Slaughter's essay "Why Women Still Can't Have It All," which appeared in the *Atlantic* in June 2012, makes some of the big-picture recommendations that Sandberg seems reluctant to articulate. Slaughter, a lawyer and the president and CEO of the New America Foundation and formerly the dean of Princeton University's Woodrow Wilson School of Public and International Affairs, wrote the essay after realizing that she would need to scale back her career to accommodate the needs of her family. After having worked in an academic setting for many years, the long hours and rigid schedule of her new position in the State Department made it very difficult for her to be present for her children, one of whom was experiencing a rocky adolescence. In the article, which had one million views in its first four days online, Slaughter asserts that it is wrong to tell young women that "having it all" is merely a "function of personal determination." Instead, she argues that individuals cannot make change alone: "It is society that must change, coming to value choices to put family ahead of work just as much as those to put work ahead of family." Slaughter advocates policies that promote flexibility at work, stating that the "default rules" about office face time need to change; working from home needs to be more acceptable, she writes, as does the practice of taking breaks in one's career. Although individuals may need to make these choices, they should feel supported by policies that do not penalize them for these decisions. In short, Slaughter states, care for others is something that needs to be acknowledged in the workplace.

Although Slaughter admits that she is writing for her own demographic—"highly educated, well-off women who are privileged enough to have choices in the first place"—all of these formulations of the work–family debate rely on a discussion about choice. The choice is something like this: Either women can choose to stay at home with their children, thereby redefining success, or they can choose to participate in market capitalism and be rewarded financially. Yet, such alternatives exist for only a very small percentage of working women. As Barbara Ehrenreich has shown in *Nickel and Dimed: On (Not) Getting By in America,* the women who found themselves unable to depend on federal assistance after the enactment of welfare reform legislation in 1996 had no such options. In fact, these women did not suddenly rise out of poverty simply because they took on low-wage jobs. Instead, women earning minimum wage barely scraped by, living hand-to-mouth, unable to afford decent housing or health care for themselves and their families. Most American workers—approximately 60 percent—make twenty dollars or less per hour, and even if they pool resources with another wage earner in their family, use housing vouchers or food stamps, or take advantage of the earned income tax credit, they rarely have enough money to break even at the end of each month, much less put something by for the next. The majority of the working population does not get to choose to "opt out"; it has to "lean in" and "get to work," whether it likes it or not.

The real issue for women in the 21st century, then, is that most women have to work, sometimes at jobs that offer deep satisfaction but more often than not at jobs that are grinding and alienating. In any case, women and their families deserve policies that help them live sane, healthy lives. Things such as paid leave for parents of new children, reliable, affordable childcare, and, to return to an example I mentioned at the beginning of the book, the ability to use a breast pump at work, should not be accessible only to those who have lucrative careers. People

Editorial cartoon that appeared in U.S. newspapers in 2007.

such as Joan Blades, the cofounder of MoveOn.org and the coauthor, with Rowe-Finkbeiner, of *The Motherhood Manifesto,* are working to organize mass support for issues connected with work-family balance. Through MomsRising.org, a website and organization they created in 2006, Blades and Rowe-Finkbeiner are generating grassroots support for family-friendly policies in upcoming elections. Organizations such as MomsRising.org show that the Christian Right can't claim exclusive ownership of "family values"; others, even liberals, are interested in revising the term so that it comes to mean a commitment to making the lives of families more equitable.

Ending this short book on the history of feminism in the United States with a reference to the Christian Right is not accidental, particularly given the fact that the right wing fueled the backlash to second wave feminism. As the nation has leaned toward conservatism in the last twenty years, the Right's opposition to abortion and gay marriage and its promotion of abstinence-only sex education programs have started to appear "normal" or unremarkable. Yet, the policies endorsed by conservatives do not reflect everyone's values, and they certainly need to be challenged to ensure that oppressed groups—women, people of color, members of the LGBT community—can live full, happy lives. One way we can challenge these policies is through the electoral process. By using the vote, something that nineteenth- and early-twentieth-century activists fought so long and hard to secure, we can honor their memories, redress the imbalances we see in society, and remake the personal and political in ways that are egalitarian and humane. Only by making our voices heard—through voting and getting involved in activist work that moves us, either locally, nationally, or globally—can we try to make changes to the policies that affect our personal and collective happiness.

READER'S GUIDE

Questions for Discussion

Do you consider yourself a feminist? Why or why not?

Were you raised in a feminist household? What aspects of your upbringing were feminist? What aspects were not?

How did this book shift your perspective on feminism?

What do you think of the wave metaphor? Is it useful? Why or why not?

What do you consider the most important gains of each wave of the feminist movement? Why?

What do you think are each wave's greatest failings or weaknesses?

What issues would you like to see the feminist movement tackle in today's world?

Media influence is everywhere. Do you think feminism has altered the portrayal of women in media (film, television, music, etc.)? If so, how?

What is or should be the role of men in the feminist movement?

Topics for Research

Pick one of the following topics and research how the situation in your state has evolved throughout the past two centuries:

Voting Rights
Questions to consider: What year did your state come into existence? When did women get the right to vote in your state? If they gained voting rights before the Nineteenth Amendment was ratified, how did this come about? What women's suffrage groups or individual activists were working on the issue in your state? Did white women and African Americans work together on suffrage issues in your state?

Politics
Questions to consider: When was the first woman elected to your state legislature? When was the first woman elected to a statewide office (for instance, as governor, secretary of state, or U.S. congressperson)? Are there groups in your state working specifically to elect women to office? How has the election of women to your state government affected legislation that has been passed?

Employment
Questions to consider: Does your state have a parental or family leave policy? If not, are legislators trying to pass such a policy? If so, what are the specifics of the policy? Who is covered and under what circumstances? How does this policy, or the lack of any policy, affect women in your state? Does it affect men differently?

Rape
Questions to consider: How does your state define rape? Has this definition changed through time? According to your state's statutes, can married women be raped by their husbands? How many women are raped each year in your state? How many of these rapes are successfully prosecuted? Are feminists in your area fighting to enact additional protections for women? What needs to change in society in order to decrease the incidence of rape?

Domestic Violence

Questions to consider: When did the first shelter open in your local area or state? How was it funded then, and how is it funded now? How many women in your state seek shelter every year? How many shelter spots are available? How many women in your state are killed by their partners (or former partners) each year? Are there specific resources in your state or city for domestic violence victims in same-sex couples?

Protest

Research a feminist strike or protest that happened in your town or state. Questions to consider: What were feminists hoping to achieve through their actions? Did they succeed? What was the town's reaction? How was the strike or protest portrayed in the local newspaper? If it were to happen today, how would the locals' reaction be the same and/ or different? How does this speak to the state of feminism in your area?

FURTHER READING AND RESOURCES

BOOKS

Anzaldúa, Gloria. *Borderlands/La frontera: The New Mestiza*. San Francisco: Aunt Lute, 1987.

Anzaldúa, Gloria, and Analouise Keating, eds. *This Bridge We Call Home: Radical Visions for Transformation*. New York: Routledge, 2002.

Aptheker, Bettina. *Intimate Politics: How I Grew Up Red, Fought for Free Speech, and Became a Feminist Rebel*. Berkeley, CA: Seal, 2006.

———. *Woman's Legacy: Essays on Race, Sex, and Class in American History*. Amherst: University of Massachusetts, 1982.

Arredondo, Gabriela F., et al., eds. *Chicana Feminisms: A Critical Reader*. Durham, NC: Duke University, 2003.

Asian Women United of California, eds. *Making Waves: An Anthology of Writings by and about Asian American Women*. Boston: Beacon, 1989.

Baker, Jean H. *Sisters: The Lives of America's Suffragists*. New York: Hill and Wang, 2005.

———, ed. *Votes for Women: The Struggle for Suffrage Revisited*. New York: Oxford University, 2002.

Banner, Lois. *Women in Modern America*. Belmont, CA: Wadsworth, 2004.

Baumgardner, Jennifer, and Amy Richards. *Grassroots: A Field Guide for Feminist Activism*. New York: Farrar, Straus and Giroux, 2004.

———. *Manifesta: Young Women, Feminism, and the Future*. New York: Farrar, Straus and Giroux, 2000.

Baxandall, Rosalyn, and Linda Gordon. *Dear Sisters: Dispatches from the Women's Liberation Movement*. New York: Basic, 2000.

Beauvoir, Simone de. *The Second Sex*. New York: Knopf, 1953.

Berry, Mary Frances. *Why ERA Failed: Politics, Women's Rights, and the Amending Process of the Constitution*. Bloomington: Indiana University, 1988.

Bolt, Christine. *Feminist Ferment: The Woman Question in the USA and England, 1870–1940*. New York: Routledge, 1995.

Brownmiller, Susan. *Against Our Will: Men, Women, and Rape*. New York: Simon and Schuster, 1975.

———. *In Our Time: Memoir of a Revolution*. New York: Dial, 1999.

Buhle, Mari Jo, and Paul Buhle, eds. *The Concise History of Woman Suffrage: Selections from the Classic Work of Stanton, Anthony, Gage, and Harper.* Urbana: University of Illinois, 1978.

Chesler, Ellen. *Woman of Valor: Margaret Sanger and the Birth Control Movement in America.* New York: Simon and Schuster, 2007.

Chopin, Kate. *The Awakening.* New York: H. S. Stone, 1899.

Collins, Patricia Hill. *Black Feminist Thought: Knowledge, Consciousness, and the Politics of Empowerment.* New York: Routledge, 1991.

Coontz, Stephanie. *A Strange Stirring: The Feminine Mystique and American Women at the Dawn of the 1960s.* New York: Basic Books, 2011.

Cott, Nancy F. *The Grounding of Modern Feminism.* New Haven: Yale University, 1987.

Crow, Barbara A., ed. *Radical Feminism: A Documentary Reader.* New York: New York University, 2000.

Davis, Angela. *Women, Race, and Class.* New York: Vintage, 1983.

Davis, Flora. *Moving the Mountain. The Women's Movement in America Since 1960.* New York: Simon and Schuster, 1991.

Deslippe, Dennis A. *Rights, Not Roses: Unions and the Rise of Working-Class Feminism, 1945–80.* Urbana: University of Illinois, 2000.

Dicker, Rory, and Alison Piepmeier, eds. *Catching a Wave: Reclaiming Feminism for the 21st Century.* Boston: Northeastern University, 2003.

Donovan, Josephine. *Feminist Theory: The Intellectual Traditions.* Third edition. New York: Continuum, 2000.

DuBois, Ellen Carol. *Woman Suffrage and Women's Rights.* New York: New York University, 1998.

———, ed. *The Elizabeth Cady Stanton–Susan B. Anthony Reader: Correspondence, Writings, Speeches.* Boston: Northeastern University, 1992.

DuPlessis, Rachel Blau, and Ann Snitow, eds. *The Feminist Memoir Project: Voices from Women's Liberation.* New York: Three Rivers, 1998.

Echols, Alice. *Daring to Be Bad: Radical Feminism in America, 1967–1975.* Minneapolis: University of Minnesota, 1989.

Evans, Sara M. *Born for Liberty: A History of Women in America.* 1989. New York: Free Press, 1997.

———. *Personal Politics: The Roots of Women's Liberation in the Civil Rights Movement and the New Left.* New York: Knopf, 1979.

———. *Tidal Wave: How Women Changed America at Century's End.* New York: Free Press, 2003.

Faderman, Lillian. *Odd Girls and Twilight Lovers: A History of Lesbian Life in Twentieth-Century America.* New York: Penguin, 1992.

Faludi, Susan. *Backlash: The Undeclared War Against American Women.* New York: Crown, 1991.

Farrell, Amy Erdman. *Yours in Sisterhood: Ms. Magazine and the Promise of Popular Feminism.* Chapel Hill: University of North Carolina, 1998.

Findlen, Barbara, ed. *Listen Up! Voices from the Next Feminist Generation.* Berkeley, CA: Seal, 2001.

Firestone, Shulamith. *The Dialectic of Sex: The Case for Feminist Revolution.* New York: Morrow, 1970.

Flexner, Eleanor. *Century of Struggle: The Woman's Rights Movement in the United States.* Cambridge, MA: Harvard University, 1973, 1996.

Freedman, Estelle B. *No Turning Back: The History of Feminism and the Future of Women.* New York: Ballantine, 2002.

Freeman, Jo. *The Politics of Women's Liberation: A Case Study of an Emerging Social Movement and Its Relation to the Policy Process.* New York: McKay, 1975.

Friedan, Betty. *The Feminine Mystique.* New York: Norton, 1963.

Garcia, Alma M., ed. *Chicana Feminist Thought: The Basic Historical Writings.* New York: Routledge, 1997.

Gilman, Charlotte Perkins. *The Yellow Wallpaper.* Boston: Small, Maynard, 1899.

Gornick, Vivian. *The Solitude of Self: Thinking About Elizabeth Cady Stanton.* New York: Farrar, Straus and Giroux, 2006.

Green, Karen, and Tristan Taormino, eds. *A Girl's Guide to Taking Over the World: Writings from the Girl Zine Revolution.* New York: St. Martin's, 1997.

Henry, Astrid. *Not My Mother's Sister: Generational Conflict and Third-Wave Feminism.* Bloomington: Indiana University, 2004.

Hernández, Daisy, and Bushra Rehman, eds. *Colonize This! Young Women of Color on Today's Feminism.* Berkeley, CA: Seal, 2002.

Heywood, Leslie, ed. *The Women's Movement Today: An Encyclopedia of Third-Wave Feminism.* 2 vols. Westport, CT: Greenwood, 2006.

Heywood, Leslie, and Jennifer Drake, eds. *Third Wave Agenda: Being Feminist, Doing Feminism.* Minneapolis: University of Minnesota, 1997.

Hine, Darlene Clark, ed. *Black Women in America.* 2nd ed. New York: Oxford University, 2005.

hooks, bell. *Ain't I a Woman: Black Women and Feminism.* Cambridge, MA: South End, 1999.

———. *Feminism Is for Everybody: Passionate Politics.* Cambridge, MA: South End, 2000.

———. *Feminist Theory: From Margin to Center.* Cambridge, MA: South End, 1984.

———. *Talking Back: Thinking Feminist, Thinking Black.* Cambridge, MA: South End, 1989.

Hull, Gloria T., Patricia Bell Scott, and Barbara Smith, eds. *All the Women Are White, All the Blacks Are Men, But Some of Us Are Brave: Black Women's Studies.* New York: Feminist Press, 1982.

Jay, Karla. *Tales of the Lavender Menace: A Memoir of Liberation.* New York: Basic, 1999.

Jervis, Lisa, and Andi Zeisler, eds. *BITCHfest: Ten Years of Cultural Criticism from the Pages of* Bitch *Magazine.* New York: Farrar, Straus and Giroux, 2006.

Johnston, Jill. *Lesbian Nation: The Feminist Solution.* New York: Simon and Schuster, 1974.

Jones, Jacqueline. *Labor of Love, Labor of Sorrow: Black Women, Work, and Family from Slavery to the Present.* New York: Basic, 1985.

Kauffman, Linda S., ed. *American Feminist Thought at Century's End: A Reader.* Oxford: Blackwell, 1993.

Keetley, Dawn, and John Pettegrew, eds. *Public Women, Public Words: A Documentary History of American Feminism.* 3 vols. New York: Madison House/Rowman and Littlefield, 1997 and 2002.

Kerber, Linda K., Alice Kessler-Harris, and Kathryn Kish Sklar, eds. *U.S. History as Women's History: New Feminist Essays.* Chapel Hill: University of North Carolina, 1995.

Kim, Elaine, ed. *Making More Waves: New Writing by Asian American Women.* Boston: Beacon, 1997.

Kimmel, Michael S., and Thomas Mosmiller, eds. *Against the Tide: Pro-Feminist Men in the United States, 1776–1990: A Documentary History.* Boston: Beacon, 1992.

Labaton, Vivien, and Dawn Lundy Martin, eds. *The Fire This Time: Young Activists and the New Feminism.* New York: Anchor, 2004.

Langley, Winston, and Vivian C. Fox, eds. *Women's Rights in the United States: A Documentary History.* Westport, CT: Praeger, 1998.

LeGates, Marlene. *In Their Time: A History of Feminism in Western Society.* New York: Routledge, 2001.

Lerner, Gerda, ed. *Black Women in White America.* New York: Random House, 1992.

Lorde, Audre. *Sister Outsider: Essays and Speeches.* Trumansburg, NY: The Crossing Press, 1984.

Love, Barbara J., and Nancy F. Cott, eds. *Feminists Who Changed America, 1963–1975.* Urbana: University of Illinois, 2006.

Mihesuah, Devon Abbott. *Indigenous American Women: Decolonization, Empowerment, Activism.* Lincoln: University of Nebraska, 2003.

Milkman, Ruth, ed. *Women, Work and Protest: A Century of U.S. Women's Labor History.* New York: Routledge and Kegan Paul, 1985.

Millett, Kate. *Sexual Politics.* Garden City, NY: Doubleday, 1970.

Mohanty, Chandra Talpade. *Feminism Without Borders: Decolonizing Theory, Practicing Solidarity.* Durham, NC: Duke University, 2003.

Moraga, Cherríe, and Gloria Anzaldúa, eds. *This Bridge Called My Back: Writings by Radical Women of Color.* Latham, NY: Kitchen Table/Women of Color Press, 1984.

Morgan, Robin, ed. *Sisterhood Is Powerful: An Anthology of Writings from the Women's Liberation Movement.* New York: Random House, 1970.

Muscio, Inga. *Cunt: A Declaration of Independence.* 2nd ed. Berkeley, CA: Seal, 2002.

Nam, Vickie, ed. *YE LL-Oh Girls! Emerging Voices Explore Culture, Identity, and Growing Up Asian American.* New York: Harper, 2001.

Nestle, Joan. *A Restricted Country.* Ithaca, NY: Firebrand, 1987.

O'Farrell, Brigid, and Joyce L. Kornbluh, eds. *Rocking the Boat: Union Women's Voices, 1915–1975.* New Brunswick, NJ: Rutgers University, 1996.

Painter, Nell Irvin. *Sojourner Truth: A Life, a Symbol.* New York: W. W. Norton, 1996.

Povich, Lynn. *The Good Girls Revolt: How the Women of Newsweek Sued Their Bosses and Changed the Workplace.* New York: Public Affairs, 2012.

Rich, Adrienne. *On Lies, Secrets, and Silence: Selected Prose, 1966–1978.* New York: W. W. Norton, 1979.

Rosen, Ruth. *The World Split Open: How the Modern Women's Movement Changed America.* New York: Viking, 2000.

Rossi, Alice S., ed. *The Feminist Papers: From Adams to de Beauvoir.* New York: Columbia University, 1973.

Roth, Benita. *Separate Roads to Feminism: Black, Chicana, and White Feminist Movements in America's Second Wave.* Cambridge, MA: Cambridge University, 2003.

Rowe-Finkbeiner, Kristin. *The F-Word: Feminism in Jeopardy.* Berkeley, CA: Seal, 2004.

Ruiz, Vicki L., and Ellen Carol DuBois, eds. *Unequal Sisters: A Multicultural Reader in U.S. Women's History.* 2nd ed. New York: Routledge, 1994.

Rupp, Leila J. and Verta Taylor. *Survival in the Doldrums: The American Women's Rights Movement, 1945 to the 1960s.* New York: Oxford University, 1987.

Schneir, Miriam, ed. *Feminism in Our Time: The Essential Writings, World War II to the Present.* New York: Vintage, 1994.

———, ed. *Feminism: The Essential Historical Writings.* New York: Vintage, 1972.

Serano, Julia. *Whipping Girl: A Transsexual Woman on Sexism and the Scapegoating of Femininity.* Berkeley, CA: Seal, 2007.

Shah, Sonia, ed. *Dragon Ladies: Asian American Feminists Breathe Fire.* Cambridge, MA: South End, 1997.

Solanas, Valerie. *SCUM Manifesto.* San Francisco: AK Press, 1996.

Stanton, Elizabeth Cady. *Eighty Years and More: Reminiscences 1815–1897, 1898.* Boston: Northeastern University, 1993.

Steinem, Gloria. *Outrageous Acts and Everyday Rebellions.* New York: Holt, Rinehart, and Winston, 1983.

Tax, Meredith. *The Rising of Women: Feminist Solidarity and Class Conflict, 1880–1917.* Urbana: University of Illinois, 2001.

Terborg-Penn, Rosalyn. *African American Women in the Struggle for the Vote, 1850–1920.* Bloomington: Indiana University, 1998.

Thom, Mary. *Inside* Ms.*: 25 Years of the Magazine and the Feminist Movement.* New York: Henry Holt, 1997.

Valenti, Jessica. *Full Frontal Feminism: A Young Woman's Guide to Why Feminism Matters.* Berkeley, CA: Seal, 2007.

Walker, Alice. *In Search of Our Mothers' Gardens: Womanist Prose.* New York: Harcourt Brace, 1983.

Willis, Ellen. *No More Nice Girls: Countercultural Essays.* Hanover, NH: Wesleyan University, 1992.

Wollstonecraft, Mary. *A Vindication of the Rights of Woman.* 1972. New York: Penguin Classics, 2004.

Woolf, Virginia. *A Room of One's Own.* New York and London: Harcourt Brace, 1929.

FILMS

American Experience: Eleanor Roosevelt. Directed by Sue Williams. Ambrica Productions, 2000.

Don't Need You: The Herstory of Riot Grrrl. Directed by Kerri Koch. Urban Cowgirl, 2006.

Emma Goldman: An Exceedingly Dangerous Woman. Directed by Mel Bucklin. PBS, 2004.

Girls Rock! Directed by Arne Johnson and Shane King. Girls Rock Productions, 2008.

Guerrillas in Our Midst. Directed by Amy Harrison. Women Make Movies, 1992.

The Hunting Ground. Directed by Kirby Dick. RADiUS-TWC, 2015.

If These Walls Could Talk. Directed by Cher and Nancy Savoca. HBO, 1996.

Iron Jawed Angels. Directed by Katja von Garnier. HBO, 2004.

I Was a Teenage Feminist. Directed by Therese Shechter. Women Make Movies, 2005.

Litany for Survival: The Life and Work of Audre Lorde. Directed by Ada Gay Griffin and Michelle Parkerson. Independent Television Service/POV, 1996.

Makers: Women Who Make America. Directed by Barak Goodman. Kunhardt McGee Productions, 2013.

Miss Representation. Directed by Jennifer Siebel Newsom. Ro*Co Films International, 2012.

The Motherhood Manifesto. Directed by Laura Pacheco. MomsRising.org, 2006.

My Feminism. Directed by Dominique Cardona and Laurie Colbert. Women Make Movies, 1997.

No More Nice Girls. Directed by Joan Braderman. Video Data Bank, 1989.

Not for Ourselves Alone: The Story of Elizabeth Cady Stanton & Susan B. Anthony. Directed by Ken Burns and Paul Barnes. PBS, 1999.

Ourselves, Our Bodies: The Feminist Movement and the Battle over Abortion. History Channel/A&E Television Networks, 1996.

Radical Harmonies. Directed by Dee Mosbacher. Woman Vision, 2002.

Reclaiming the Body: Feminist Art in America. Directed by Michael Blackwood. Blackwood Productions, 1995.

The Righteous Babes. Directed by Pratibha Parmar. Agran Barton Television/Women Make Movies, 1998.

She's Beautiful When She's Angry. Directed by Mary Dore. Cinema Guild, 2014.

Some American Feminists. Directed by Luce Guilbeault, Nicole Brossard, and Margaret Wescott. Women Make Movies, 1977.

Step by Step: Building a Feminist Movement, 1941–1977. Produced by Joyce Follet. Wisconsin Public Television/Step by Step, 1998.

Susan B. Anthony: Rebel for the Cause. Directed by Adam Friedman. A&E Biography, 2005.

Womanhouse. Directed by Johanna Demetrakas. Women Make Movies, 1974.

WEBSITES

American Women: A Gateway to Library of Congress Resources for the Study of Women's History and Culture in the United States: http://lcweb2.loc.gov/ammem/awhhtml

American Women's History: A Research Guide, Archives and Manuscript Collections: http://frank.mtsu.edu/~kmiddlet/history/women/wh-manu.html

The Emma Goldman Papers Project: http://sunsite.berkeley.edu/Goldman

The Equal Rights Amendment: www.4era.org

Feminist Studies Collections: Internet Resources:http://library.stanford.edu/depts/ssrg/kkerns/feminist.html

The Lesbian Herstory Archives: www.lesbianherstoryarchives.org

The Lucretia Coffin Mott Papers Project: www.mott.pomona.edu

The Margaret Sanger Papers Project: www.nyu.edu/projects/sanger

Ms. Foundation for Women: http://ms.foundation.org

National American Woman Suffrage Association Collection: http://memory.loc.gov/ammem/naw/nawshome.html

National Museum of Women's History: www.nmwh.org

National Organization for Women: www.now.org

National Women's History Project: www.nwhp.org

National Women's Law Center: www.nwlc.org

Third Wave Foundation: www.thirdwavefoundation.org

The Triangle Factory Fire: www.ilr.cornell.edu/trianglefire

WMST-L Women's Studies Listserv:
    http://userpages.umbc.edu/~Korenman/wmst/wmst-l.html

SOURCES

Chapter 1

Cott, Nancy F. *The Grounding of Modern Feminism.* New Haven, CT: Yale University, 1987.

Davis, Flora. *Moving the Mountain: The Women's Movement in America Since 1960.* New York: Simon and Schuster, 1991.

Douglas, Susan J. *Where the Girls Are: Growing Up Female with the Mass Media.* New York: Times Books, 1994.

Echols, Alice. *Daring to Be Bad: Radical Feminism in America, 1967–1975.* Minneapolis: University of Minnesota, 1989.

Evans, Sara M. *Tidal Wave: How Women Changed America at Century's End.* New York: Free Press, 2003.

Faludi, Susan. *Backlash: The Undeclared War Against American Women.* New York: Crown, 1991.

Freedman, Estelle B. *No Turning Back: The History of Feminism and the Future of Women.* New York: Ballantine, 2002.

Friedan, Betty. *It Changed My Life: Writings on the Women's Movement.* New York: Random House, 1976.

hooks, bell. *Feminism Is for Everybody: Passionate Politics.* Cambridge, MA: South End, 2000.
———. *Feminist Theory: From Margin to Center.* Cambridge, MA: South End, 1984.

Hymowitz, Carol, and Michaele Weissman. *A History of Women in America.* New York: Bantam, 1978.

Jordan, June. *Civil Wars.* Boston: Beacon, 1981.

Matthews, Jean V. *The Rise of the New Woman: The Women's Movement in America, 1875–1930.* Chicago: Ivan R. Dee, 2003.

Moraga, Cherríe. *Loving in the War Years.* Boston: South End, 1983.

Moraga, Cherríe, and Gloria Anzaldúa, eds. *This Bridge Called My Back: Writings by Radical Women of Color.* New York: Kitchen Table/Women of Color Press, 1984.

Morgan, Robin, ed. *Sisterhood Is Powerful: An Anthology of Writings from the Women's Liberation Movement.* New York: Random House, 1970.

Papazian, Ellen. "Women of the Verge." *Ms.,* November 1996.

Quindlen, Anna. "And Now, Babe Feminism." *New York Times,* January 19, 1994.

Rowe-Finkbeiner, Kristin. *The F-Word: Feminism in Jeopardy.* Berkeley, CA: Seal, 2004.

Siegel, Deborah. *Sisterhood, Interrupted: From Radical Women to Grrls Gone Wild.* New York: Palgrave Macmillan, 2007.

Smith, Barbara. "Racism and Women's Studies." *The Truth That Never Hurts: Writings on Race, Gender, and Freedom.* New Brunswick, NJ: Rutgers University, 1998.

Stanton, Elizabeth Cady, Susan B. Anthony, and Matilda Joslyn Gage, eds. *The History of Woman Suffrage.* New York: Fowler and Wells, 1881.

West, Rebecca. "Mr. Chesterton in Hysterics: A Study in Prejudice," *The Clarion,* November 14, 1913.

Chapter 2

Baker, Jean H., ed. *Votes for Women: The Struggle for Suffrage Revisited.* New York: Oxford University, 2002.

DuBois, Ellen Carol. *Woman Suffrage and Women's Rights.* New York: New York University, 1998.

Flexner, Eleanor. *Century of Struggle: The Woman's Rights Movement in the United States.* Cambridge, MA: Harvard University, 1973, 1996.

Hymowitz, Carol, and Michaele Weissman. *A History of Women in America.* New York: Bantam, 1978.

Kleinberg, S. J. *Women in the United States, 1830–1945.* New Brunswick, NJ: Rutgers University, 1999.

Matthews, Jean V. *The Rise of the New Woman: The Women's Movement in America, 1875–1930.* Chicago: Ivan R. Dee, 2003.

Rossi, Alice S., ed. *The Feminist Papers: From Adams to de Beauvoir.* New York: Columbia University, 1973.

Stanton, Elizabeth Cady, Susan B. Anthony, and Matilda Joslyn Gage, eds. *The History of Woman Suffrage.* New York: Fowler and Wells, 1881.

Ward, Geoffrey C. *Not for Ourselves Alone: The Story of Elizabeth Cady Stanton and Susan B. Anthony.* New York: Knopf, 1999.

Chapter 3

Berkeley, Kathleen C. *The Women's Liberation Movement in America.* Westport, CT: Greenwood, 1999.

Brownmiller, Susan. *In Our Time: Memoir of a Revolution.* New York: Dial, 1999.

Cobble, Dorothy Sue, Linda Gordon, and Astrid Henry. *Feminism Unfinished: A Short, Surprising History of American Women's Movements.* New York: Liveright, 2014.

Dow, Bonnie J. "Feminism, Miss America, and Media Mythology." *Rhetoric and Public Affairs* 7 (2003): 127–60.

Echols, Alice. *Daring to Be Bad: Radical Feminism in America, 1967–1975.* Minneapolis: University of Minnesota, 1989.

Evans, Sara M. *Personal Politics: The Roots of Women's Liberation in the Civil Rights Movement and the New Left.* New York: Knopf, 1979.

———. *Tidal Wave: How Women Changed America at Century's End.* New York: Free Press, 2003.

Friedan, Betty. *The Feminine Mystique.* New York: Norton, 1963.

Hanisch, Carol. "The Personal Is Political," *Notes from the Second Year.* Shulamith Firestone and Anne Koedt, eds. New York: Radical Feminism, 1970.

Hymowitz, Carol, and Michaele Weissman. *A History of Women in America.* New York: Bantam, 1978.

Le Sueur, Meridel. *Ripening: Selected Work, 1927–1980.* Old Westbury, NY: Feminist Press, 1982.

Morgan, Robin, ed. *Sisterhood Is Powerful: An Anthology of Writings from the Women's Liberation Movement.* New York: Random House, 1970.

Rosen, Ruth. *How the Modern Women's Movement Changed America.* New York: Viking, 2000.

Rupp, Leila J., and Verta Taylor. *Survival in the Doldrums: The American Women's Rights Movement, 1945 to the 1960s.* New York: Oxford University, 1987.

Ryan, Barbara. *Feminism and the Women's Movement: Dynamics of Change in Social Movement Ideology and Activism.* New York: Routledge, 1992.

Tobias, Sheila. *Faces of Feminism: An Activist's Reflections on the Women's Movement.* Boulder CO: Westview, 1997.

Walker, Nancy A. *Shaping Our Mothers' World: American Women's Magazines.* Jackson: University Press of Mississippi, 2000.

Chapter 4

Baumgardner, Jennifer, and Amy Richards. *Manifesta: Young Women, Feminism, and the Future.* New York: Farrar, Straus and Giroux, 2000.

Berkeley, Kathleen C. *The Women's Liberation Movement in America.* Westport, CT: Greenwood, 1999.

Bolotin, Susan. "Voices from the Post-Feminist Generation." *New York Times Magazine,* October 17, 1982.

Damsky, Lee, ed. *Sex and Single Girls: Straight and Queer Women on Sexuality.* Berkeley: Seal, 2000.

Dicker, Rory, and Alison Piepmeier, eds. *Catching a Wave: Reclaiming Feminism for the 21st Century.* Boston: Northeastern University, 2003.

Douglas, Susan J. *Where the Girls Are: Growing Up Female with the Mass Media.* New York: Times Books, 1994.

Evans, Sara M. *Tidal Wave: How Women Changed America at Century's End.* New York: Free Press, 2003.

Faludi, Susan. *Backlash: The Undeclared War Against American Women.* New York: Crown, 1991.

Findlen, Barbara, ed. *Listen Up: Voices from the Next Feminist Generation.* Berkeley, CA: Seal, 2001.

Gillis, Stacy, Gillian Howie, and Rebecca Munford, eds. *Third Wave Feminism : A Critical Exploration.* New York: Palgrave Macmillan, 2004.

Heywood, Leslie, ed. *The Women's Movement Today: An Encyclopedia of Third-Wave Feminism.* Westport, CT: Greenwood, 2006.

Heywood, Leslie, and Jennifer Drake, eds. *Third Wave Agenda: Being Feminist, Doing Feminism.* Minneapolis: University of Minnesota, 1997.

Kamen, Paula. *Feminist Fatale: Voices from the "Twentysomething" Generation Explore the Future of the "Women's Movement."* New York: Donald I. Fine, 1991.

Moraga, Cherríe, and Gloria Anzaldúa, eds. *This Bridge Called My Back: Writings by Radical Women of Color.* New York: Kitchen Table/Women of Color Press, 1984.

Reger, Jo., ed. *Different Wavelengths: Studies of the Contemporary Women's Movement.* New York: Routledge, 2005.

Valenti, Jessica. *Full Frontal Feminism: A Young Woman's Guide to Why Feminism Matters.* Berkeley, CA: Seal, 2007.

Walker, Alice. *In Search of Our Mothers' Gardens: Womanist Prose.* New York: Harcourt Brace, 1983.

Walker, Rebecca. "Becoming the Third Wave." *Ms.,* January/February 1992.

———, ed. *To Be Real: Telling the Truth and Changing the Face of Feminism.* New York: Anchor, 1995.

Whittier, Nancy. *Feminist Generations: The Persistence of the Radical Women's Movement.* Philadelphia: Temple University, 1995.

Wolf, Naomi. *The Beauty Myth: How Images of Beauty Are Used Against Women.* New York: Morrow, 1991.

Chapter 5

Baumgardner, Jennifer. *F'em! Goo Goo, Gaga, and Some Thoughts on Balls.* Berkeley, CA: Seal, 2011.

Belkin, Lisa. "The Opt-Out Revolution." *New York Times Magazine,* October 26, 2003.

Brownmiller, Susan. *In Our Time: Memoir of a Revolution.* New York: Dial, 1999.

Ehrenreich, Barbara. *Nickel and Dimed: On (Not) Getting by in America.* New York: Metropolitan Books, 2001.

Hirshman, Linda R. *Get to Work: A Manifesto for Women of the World.* New York: Viking, 2006.

Hogeland, Lisa Maria. "Fear of Feminism: Why Young Women Get the Willies." *Ms.,* November/December 1994.

Jervis, Lisa. "The End of Feminism's Third Wave." *Ms.,* Winter 2004/2005.

Kimmel, Michael. "Real Men Join the Movement." *Ms.,* November/December 1997.

Richards, Amelia (Amy). "Body Image: Third Wave Feminism's Issue?" In *Body Outlaws: Rewriting the Rules of Beauty and Body Image,* edited by Ophira Edut, 196–200. Berkeley, CA: Seal, 1998.

Riley, Sirena J. "The Black Beauty Myth." In *Colonize This! Young Women of Color on Today's Feminism,* edited by Daisy Hernández and Bushra Rehman, 357–69. Berkeley, CA: Seal, 2002.

Rowe-Finkbeiner, Kristin. *The F-Word: Feminism in Jeopardy.* Berkeley, CA: Seal, 2004.

Sandberg, Sheryl. *Lean In: Women, Work, and the Will to Lead.* New York: Knopf, 2013.

Seidman, Rachel F. "Who Needs Feminism? Lessons from a Digital World." *Feminist Studies* 39.2 (2013): 549-62.

Slaughter, Anne-Marie. "Why Women Still Can't Have It All." *Atlantic Monthly,* July/August 2012.

Wolf, Naomi. *The Beauty Myth: How Images of Beauty Are Used Against Women.* New York: Morrow, 1991.

INDEX

A

abolitionism: activists for 32–34; feminism as coincident with 26–29; Truth, Sojourner 32–33; women-only groups 25–26

abortion: before *Roe v. Wade* 86; Redstockings protest 85–86; reversal of gains on 105; *Roe v. Wade* 86–87; violence against clinics 105–107

About-face.org: 147

Addams, Jane: 52–54

Adichie, Chimimanda Ngozi: xv

advertising: protesting sexist 145, 147; sex-segregated 69, 74; *see also* media, the

affirmative action: 74, 104

African-American feminists: vs. Anglo-centric radicals 91–92; on body image 146; as exempt from the second wave 82; movements among 91–93; third wave 109; as womanists 110–111

African-American women, 19th century: 24

Against Our Will: Men, Women, and Rape (Brownmiller): 88

A Girl Like Me (Davis): 146

AIDS activism: 114–116

AIDS Coalition to Unleash Power (ACT UP): 115–116

All the Women Are White, All the Blacks Are Men, But Some of Us Are Brave (Hull, Scott, and Smith): 109

American Equal Rights Association (AERA): 39, 40

American Woman Suffrage Association (AWSA): 41, 44

Anthony, Susan B.: on abolitionism 28; friendship with Stanton 35–36; as president of NAWSA 44; suffrage activism by 38–40; on Victoria Woodhull 43

Anthony Amendment: 47, 54–55

antiabortion groups: 105

Anzaldúa, Gloria: 109

art world, sexism in the: 112–113

athletics: 98

Atkinson, Ti-Grace: 75, 88

Auclert, Hubertine: 10

The Awakening (Chopin): 9

B

"back alley" abortions: 96

Backlash: The Undeclared War Against American Women (Faludi): 19, 104

Baumgardner, Jennifer: 140–141

beauty ideals: of girlie feminists 122; historical changes in 145–146; Miss America protest 83–84; and need for ongoing activism 3, 6–7, 145–147

Belkin, Lisa: 152

Beyoncé: xv

Bikini Kill: 119

ACKNOWLEDGMENTS

I would first like to thank Krista Lyons for the invitation to update *A History of U.S. Feminisms*. Thanks are due as well to the staff at Seal—Laura Mazer, Eva Zimmerman, Sarah Juckniess, Anna Gallagher, and Ashley Redfield—for their enthusiasm and efficiency in the production and publicity processes.

It is gratifying to know that this book has found a place in the world and will continue to reach an audience. I appreciate those who have told me that this book has been helpful to them: students, colleagues, friends, and strangers.

I would also like to thank the staff at the Margaret Cuninggim Women's Center—Alex Hollifield, Emily Hickey, Brenda Caplinger, Kinsey Walker, and Briana Perry—for their interest in the project and their understanding of my deadlines. I also would like to thank Pat Helland for recognizing my commitment to this revision even as I was stepping into a new role at the Women's Center.

My family has supported me through this revision, even as it coincided with the demands of a new job. I want to thank my husband, Paul DeHart, for his encouragement and love, as well as my mother, Ellen Dicker, for her enthusiasm and help. Both Paul and my mother took on additional childcare and domestic duties as I worked on this project; I could not have accomplished this revision without them. I also want to acknowledge my daughters Alice and Delia. Although they are too young now to understand the ins and outs of feminist history, I look forward to the time when I can share these stories with them.

Although it seems long ago now, I remember imagining how this book should sound as I worked on the first edition. The idea of writing the book in the style of a lecture struck me as the perfect tone for this book. It also situated this book—and me—in the classroom, where I feel most at home. As I wrote, I imagined that I was speaking to my students, whom I wish to thank here for insights that continue to amaze me; their ideas and energy teach me new ways of thinking about feminism, particularly in its most recent incarnations.

ABOUT THE AUTHOR

A native of New York State, RORY DICKER
completed her undergraduate studies at the
Johns Hopkins University in Baltimore,
Maryland, and earned her M.A. and Ph.D.
in English from Vanderbilt University, in
Nashville, Tennessee. After teaching for
several years at Westminster College in
Fulton, Missouri, she returned to Nashville,
where she lives with her husband and two
daughters. She teaches classes about women
and literature, feminist pedagogy, and the
history of American feminisms at Vanderbilt
University, where she is the Director of the
Margaret Cuninggim Women's Center. She is the coeditor of *Catching
a Wave: Reclaiming Feminism for the 21st Century*.

photo by Anne Rayner, Vanderbilt.

CREDITS

Chapter 1

"If I Had a Hammer, I'd Smash Patriarchy" cartoon, artist unknown, was provided by Microcosm Publishing.

"Women of the World Unite," photograph by Fred W. McDarrah, is reprinted with permission. © Gloria S. McDarrah.

Excerpt from *Sisterhood Is Powerful,* ©1970 by Robin Morgan, is reprinted by permission of Edite Kroll Literary Agency Inc.

Chapter 2

Sojourner Truth image was provided by the Library of Congress.

Elizabeth Cady Stanton and Susan B. Anthony image was provided by the Library of Congress.

"Two more bright spots on the map," by Harry Osborn, appeared on the front page of the *Maryland Suffrage News,* Vol. III, No. 33, Saturday November 14, 1914, and is reprinted by permission of the Maryland Historical Society.

"The First Picket Line" image from the National Woman's Party records was provided by the Library of Congress.

"The Sky Is Now Her Limit," by Bushnell, originally appeared in the *New York Times Monthly Magazine* in 1920 and was provided by the Library of Congress.

Chapter 3

Meridel Le Sueur excerpt from "Women Know a Lot of Things" in *Ripening: Selected Work, Second Edition.* © 1937, © 1975 by Meridel Le Sueur. Reprinted with the permission of the Feminist Press at the City University of New York, www.feministpress .org. All rights reserved.

Rosie the Riveter image (by artist J. Howard Miller) #798 from *War And Conflict* was provided by the National Archives.

National Organization for Women organizing conference photo was provided by and is reproduced with permission of the National Organization for Women.

Miss America protest photo was provided by and is reprinted with the permission of the Associated Press.

Barbara Smith, Audre Lorde, Cherríe Moraga, and Hattie Gossett in Kitchen Table Press T-shirts, © 2007 JEB (Joan E. Biren). Reprinted by permission of the photographer.

Rita Mae Brown photograph by Diana Davies appeared in *In Our Time* by Susan Brownmiller and is reprinted with permission of the New York Public Library.

Excerpts from Sara M. Evans's *Tidal Wave* are reprinted with the permission of the Free Press, a division of Simon & Schuster Adult Publishing Group. © 2003 by Sara M. Evans. All rights reserved.

Chapter 4

"Womanist" from *In Search Of Our Mother's Gardens: Womanist Prose*, © 1983 by Alice Walker, is reprinted by permission of Harcourt, Inc.

"Do Women Have to be Naked to Get into U.S. Museums?" © by Guerrilla Girls, Inc. 2007. Reprinted by permission of Guerrilla Girls, Inc.

"The Eco-feminist Imperative (May 1981)" by Ynestra King. *Reclaim the Earth: Women Speak Out for Life on Earth.* Eds. Leonie Caldecott and Stephanie Leland. Reprinted courtesy of the Women's Press, London, 1993.

Photograph of women elected to Senate in 1992, reprinted courtesy of the Office of U.S. Senator Dianne Feinstein.

Excerpt from *Off Our Backs* Volume 12, Number 4, April 1982 by Cherríe Moraga, © 1982. All rights reserved.

Excerpt from *This Bridge Called My Back: Writings by Radical Women Of Color,* edited by Cherríe Moraga and Gloria Anzaldúa © 1984. All rights reserved.

Excerpt from *To Be Real: Telling the Truth and Changing the Face of Feminism,* by Rebecca Walker © 1984. Reprinted with permission from Random House Inc. All rights reserved.

Radical cheer lyrics from "Queerleader" and "Riot, Don't Diet" are reprinted by permission of the New York City Radical Cheerleaders (NYCRC).

Lickity Split Radical Cheerleaders, Chicago is provided courtesy of Julie Freburg.

Chapter 5

Excerpt from Lisa Jervis's speech, as it appeared in *Ms.* magazine, reprinted courtesy of *Ms.* magazine.

"We're the Only Childcare Your Mom Can Afford" cartoon reprinted by permission of Mike Luckovich and Creators Syndicate, Inc.

SELECTED TITLES FROM SEAL PRESS

For more than thirty years, Seal Press has published groundbreaking books. By women. For women. Visit our website at www.sealpress.com and our blog at www.sealpress.com/blog.

Transgender History by Susan Stryker. $12.95, 1-58005-224-X. An introduction to transgender history from the mid–19th century through today.

Listen Up: Voices from the Next Feminist Generation edited by Barbara Findlen. $16.95, 1-58005-054-9. A collection of essays featuring the voices of today's young feminists on racism, sexuality, identity, AIDS, revolution, abortion, and much more.

Colonize This: Young Women of Color on Today's Feminism edited by Daisy Hernández and Bushra Rehman. $16.95, 1-58005-067-0. An insight into a new generation of brilliant, outspoken women of color, how they are speaking to the concerns of a new feminism, and their place in it.

Intimate Politics: How I Grew Up Red, Fought for Free Speech, and Became a Feminist Rebel by Bettina F. Aptheker. $16.95, 1-58005-160-X. A courageous and uncompromising account of one woman's personal and political transformation, and a fascinating portrayal of a key chapter in our nation's history.

The Maternal Is Political: Women Writers at the Intersection of Motherhood and Social Change edited by Shari MacDonald Strong. $15.95, 1-58005-243-6. Exploring the vital connection between motherhood and social change, *The Maternal Is Political* features thirty powerful literary essays by women striving to make the world a better place for children and families—both their own and other women's.

Nobody Passes: Rejecting the Rules of Gender and Conformity edited by Mattilda a.k.a Matt Bernstein Sycamore. $15.95, 1-58005-184-7. A timely and thought-provoking collection of essays that confronts and challenges the notion of belonging by examining the perilous intersections of identity, categorization, and community.